CRYING IN THE WILDERNESS

The Struggle for Justice in South Africa

Archbishop Desmond Tutu

Edited and introduced by
JOHN WEBSTER

Foreword by

The Most Reverend
Trevor Huddleston, CR

WM. B. EERDMANS PUBLISHING CO.
GRAND RAPIDS, MICHIGAN

Published in the United States of America by
Wm. B. Eerdmans Publishing Company
255 Jefferson S.E., Grand Rapids, MI 49503

Published in Great Britain by Mowbray, a Cassell imprint

Introduction and notes © John Webster 1982, 1986, 1990
Text © Desmond Tutu 1982, 1986, 1990

First published 1982 as *Bishop Desmond Tutu: the Voice of One Crying in
the Wilderness*
Second edition 1986 as *Desmond Tutu: Crying in the Wilderness*
This edition first published 1990

Library of Congress Cataloging in Publication Data

Tutu, Desmond
   Crying in the wilderness.
   Bibliography: p. 124.
   1.   South Africa — Race relations — Addresses,
essays, lectures.   2.   Church and race
relations — South Africa — Addresses, essays,
lectures.   3.   South African Council of
Churches — Addresses, essays, lectures.
4.   South Africa — Church history — Addresses,
essays, lectures.
I.   Webster, John   II. Title.
DT763.T88   1982   261.8'348'00968   82-7449
ISBN 0-8028-0270-2   AACR2

Typeset by Area Graphics Ltd, Letchworth, Herts

Printed and bound in Great Britain by
Mackays of Chatham PLC, Chatham, Kent

No man is an island intire of it selfe;
Every man is a peece of the Continent,
a part of the maine

JOHN DONNE

Note

At the time of the first edition of this book Desmond Tutu was Bishop of Johannesburg. He is therefore frequently so described in the text, before his election in 1986 as Archbishop of Cape Town.

Foreword

It is now nearly ten years since I wrote the Foreword to the first edition of this book: it is time for a reassessment of Desmond Tutu's influence on events in South Africa. As winner of the Nobel Peace Prize and first black Archbishop of Cape Town he has become a world figure and his place in the history of his country and his Church is assured.

But this is certainly not the moment for any final judgement on the impact of this remarkable man on the rapidly changing scene in South Africa. What I shall attempt, therefore, is an informal comment at the present moment (1990), based on a friendship of some forty years, on the work of one who is at the height of his power and still young. Perhaps one of the two blessings of old age is that it brings with it a long perspective, and, I hope, a respect for history itself. It certainly brings with it, for me, the most vivid memories of my life and of the people who gave me their friendship and their trust.

When Desmond was a small boy he had nearly two years in hospital, suffering from tuberculosis: two crucial years when he should have been in school preparing for matriculation. As the clinic was quite close to Sophiatown and the Priory of the Community of the Resurrection where I lived, I was able to visit him very frequently. When he recovered and went back to school he stayed for a while in our small hostel. So I suppose I can claim to have seen him at a very critical period of his life: an adolescence, with more than its usual strains and stresses, against the background of a South Africa of increasing turbulence. Desmond was seventeen when the present Nationalist Government came to power in 1948: I was recalled and left the country (as I thought for good) eight years later.

It was during those eight years that all the major legislation imposing 'apartheid' on the whole nation was passed. Every law not only strengthened existing racist structures but imposed a system reaching out into every area of life, social, economic, cultural, political and even religious. Every African was caught up in this process and imprisoned by it in a seemingly inescapable serfdom. But none more so than the highly gifted and intelligent young, like Desmond himself, who knew that the purpose of apartheid was their total exclusion from citizenship in their own land. Dr Verwoerd, architect of 'grand apartheid' and creator of most of its laws, spelt this out very clearly when he introduced the Bantu Education Act with the words: 'Education, for the native, exists to equip him for certain forms of labour. There are green pastures in which he has no right to graze.'

As Desmond, in his education and in response to vocation in the Church's ministry, experienced the consequences of apartheid, he articulated the challenge again and again. This book is the expression of that challenge.

'A time of crisis is not just a time of anxiety and worry. It gives a chance, an opportunity, to choose well or to choose badly. You have to decide which way you want to go. . . .' Through the years, as Secretary General of the South African Council of Churches; as Dean, and later, Bishop of Johannesburg, and finally, as Archbishop of Cape Town, Desmond was faced with crisis after crisis. His voice was heard above the tumult with the unceasing challenge 'Please let us move away from the edge of the precipice. God is giving us perhaps our last chance'—Reconciliation; yes. But reconciliation without justice is impossible.

It has been his unwavering insistence on the Gospel truth, that, in society, Love itself is expressed in Justice and is meaningless without it, that has given to Desmond the authenticity which gives him his authority. It has also made him many enemies. His support for sanctions, particularly economic sanctions, as required by the United Nations resolutions, has been bitterly resented not only by white South Africans, but by some black leaders also. Yet he repeatedly stated that the only purpose of sanctions is to put pressure on the regime in Pretoria so that it will be compelled to abandon and destroy apartheid if it wishes to avoid a blood-bath. Sanctions is in fact the only non-violent alternative to civil war.

Today, as a result of President de Klerk's speech on 2 February 1990, 'the wind of change' in South Africa, so long ago proclaimed by Harold Macmillan and so long resisted, has begun to blow. With the unbanning of the African National Congress and other organisations: with the release of Nelson Mandela and some others serving life-sentences: with the promise of an end to the State of Emergency—the door appears to be open to meaningful negotiations between the black majority leadership and the white minority regime.

In a Pastoral Letter to his people in the Diocese of Cape Town in February 1990, after the release of Nelson Mandela, Desmond wrote: 'The road ahead may be long and hazardous but at long last it seems that what so many have prayed and fasted for, sacrificed and died for, were imprisoned, banned and went into exile for, at long last it seems more attainable than ever before'.

And, in answering an interviewer from an overseas television service on 11 February, *after* Mandela's release, when asked 'Are there any potential dangers in the process (of negotiation)?' he answered: 'Of course, you might have intransigence on one side or the other. . . . But my own feeling is, let's get these talks under way, because when people sit down to talk to each other, they begin to discover each other.' In answer to another interviewer about his own role in the future: 'I have said that I am going to adopt a lower profile . . . we had to fulfil a role . . . because our real leaders were either in jail or in exile . . . I am not a politician . . . I am a pastor. I am a pastor. . . .'

But, whether a pastor or a prophet, he is still held within an imprisoned society. Apartheid is still in place. Not one single apartheid law (as I write these words in March 1990) has been repealed. And every day that the apartheid structures remain in place they destroy people made in the image and likeness of God. The negotiating process must be swift and positive if the long night is to end and the 'crying in the wilderness' is to be silenced with an 'Alleluia!' I have no doubt that freedom will come to South Africa. I pray that I may see it before I die.

For Desmond there is still vital work to do, and he will do it, as he has done in the past, in loving obedience to the Lord he serves.

16 March 1990   THE RT REVD TREVOR HUDDLESTON, CR

Contents

Editor's Preface

THIS COLLECTION of Bishop Tutu's sermons, speeches, articles and press statements documents a lively two-and-half years in the life of the South African Council of Churches, from Bishop Tutu's appointment as General Secretary on 1 March 1978, to the abortive meeting between the SACC and the South African Prime Minister and government in August 1980. The material is arranged so that Part One covers the general theoretical background, Part Two the practical work of the SACC, and Part Three the South African situation. Part Four deals with the forces of change in the country, and Part Five opens out into a look at the world, and the future role of the Church in it. A few of the pieces have been run together from several sources that all deal with the same subject; others have been extracted from a speech or address and reprinted under a sub-heading. Wherever possible the date has been given, and notes added to give the background and explain references.

I would like to thank everybody who has helped me with this book. Special thanks are due to the Revd Brian Brown, Africa Secretary of the British Council of Churches, who has read and corrected the manuscript and made many valuable suggestions, as well as providing detailed information for the notes. I would also like to thank the staff of the USPG library, Westminster, for their help with research, and to Mowbray's Publishing Division for the consistent encouragement they have given. Finally I would like to thank my father, Alan Webster, who set this book in motion.

J.W.

Preface to the second edition

This second edition reprints the original text with a few minor changes, together with a revised introduction, and a new Part Six, bringing the book up-to-date with a final chapter, which contains the edited text of an address given by Bishop Tutu at the Royal Commonwealth Society in London on 7 October 1985, and has been made available by courtesy of the Royal Commonwealth Society.

June 1986   J.W.

Preface to the third edition

This third edition has been updated by the addition of new material to Part Six, and developments in South Africa and the life of Desmond Tutu have been traced in the revised introduction and in the editorial notes to the final section. Minor revisions have also been made in the editorial notes.

I would like to thank all those who have helped: Canon Stephen Platten, Martin Wattam of the UN Information Centre, Alison Webb of Marble Arch Productions, and Slavia Gonzalez of the Anglican Consultative Council; also Revd Brian Brown, who has again assisted with detailed information about South Africa.

The resolutions from the 1988 Lambeth Conference are © The Secretary General of the Anglican Consultative Council 1988.

J.W.

Introduction

THE AWARD of the Nobel Peace Prize to Desmond Tutu in 1984 was a fit recognition of his efforts to bring a non-violent transition to majority rule in South Africa. In a vivid energetic land his voice is one of wisdom, which speaks of a path to a society where these energies can be channelled into creativity rather than violence. 'Trying to be a little bit of a visionary', as he puts it, he none the less refuses to retreat into otherworldliness; his witness, as can be seen from the writings and speeches from his time as General Secretary of the South African Council of Churches, is strikingly practical, and is as likely to come in the form of a press statement concerning evictions as a sermon from the pulpit. The consistent sense of the obscenity of apartheid is carried onto the world stage in the speeches and statements also collected here, after the award of the Nobel Peace Prize to the end of the 1980s.

In 1986, when he was elected Archbishop of Cape Town, Desmond Tutu became the most senior Anglican Churchman in South Africa. Soon he began to try to bring democratic processes into the mainstream of South African life, marching out from his Cathedral in Cape Town, trying to dispel the accusations of treason that the South African government has always levelled at non-violent protests. His courage is undoubted and sometimes breathtaking, and such courage is infectious; 'he is everything a leader should be' said one of his colleagues, referring to the variety of weapons that he brings to the struggle against apartheid: bravery, vision, intellect, charisma. For the black South Africans he has become a symbol of hope, a man who speaks with their voice and pits his whole being against the hated system of apartheid.

The system of apartheid was embarked upon in 1948—the white minority government 'elected' in that year built upon the discriminatory practices they inherited, and constructed a philosophical and theological edifice under which their policy of self interest and naked racism could be sheltered. The role of the black population was to serve the white population whilst being educated as slaves: the Group Areas Act and the Bantu Education

Act, enacted during the 1950s, put this low-minded and grossly selfish policy into effect. The black population reacted with a series of peaceful protests which were repressed with increasing violence, culminating in the notorious Sharpeville massacre of 1960, when 69 people were shot dead during a peaceful protest against the Pass Laws. Following this massacre the leading black opposition party, the African National Congress (ANC), whose aim is to achieve a non-racial democracy in South Africa based on the 1955 Freedom Charter, came to the bleak realisation that their policy of non-violent resistance had not brought the day of freedom any closer, and in 1961 they set up an armed wing—Umkhonto we Sizwe (Spear of the Nation). The 1960s saw the minority government building up an armoury of increasingly repressive laws which outlawed black political opinion, and subjected opponents of apartheid to grim persecutions. During the 1970s the movement of the black population towards armed struggle was given further momentum after the Soweto riots of 1976, a development which continued into the 1980s. Though certain reforms took place during this period, they did not address the central political demand of the black population—majority rule—and failed to resolve South Africa's political crisis.

During the 1960s Church opposition to apartheid became more vocal—conferences of the World Council of Churches (WCC) formulated a firmer Christian response, and in 1970 the WCC announced that it was making funds available to the South African liberation movements, the ANC and the Pan Africanist Congress (PAC)—organisations which had turned to the armed struggle after Sharpeville. Though the Church grants were not for arms, but for social services and medical supplies, the decision to make the grants caused enormous controversy. The SACC was immediately threatened with dire consequences by the then Prime Minister Mr Vorster if it did not withdraw from the WCC; at a tense meeting the SACC nevertheless decided against withdrawal, but to repudiate the use of violence as a means of bringing about social change. The government reaction was to refuse visas to anyone connected with the World Council, and to prevent the SACC sending funds to it.

So by the early 1970s the difference of opinion between Church and State in South Africa over the central issue of apartheid had become much more clearly defined. It was against this background that Desmond Tutu emerged in the mid-1970s as one of South Africa's most articulate and effective Christians. In 1975 he was appointed Dean of Johannesburg—the first black person to hold this office—and following the Soweto riots of 1976 he rose to prominence as a commentator on the South African situation. In 1977 he was appointed General Secretary of the SACC, from where he repeatedly challenged the thinking and policies of the practitioners of apartheid, and spoke up forcefully for the oppressed black majority, steadfast in his espousal of majority rule. Under his leadership the SACC provided legal aid for many political prisoners and financial assistance for their families. This clear response to apartheid was infused with his qualities of great personal courage, his desire for good relations between the races, and last but not least, his unique sense of humour, sometimes described as 'impish'.

Desmond Tutu was born on 7 October 1931, in Klerksdorp, a town in the Western Transvaal, seventy miles west of Johannesburg. His father was a Methodist schoolteacher, headmaster of a local primary school and his mother was a domestic worker who had a strongly marked tendency to side with the underdog. Their newly born son was not expected to live long, but he survived and was given the middle name Mpilo—meaning 'Life' at his baptism. Desmond was educated at a Swedish mission school at Roodeport, and then attended a secondary school for blacks. From these years he remembers sad realities of life in South Africa: the racial taunts from white boys, the black children scavenging in the school dustbins for food, and the humiliation of going to a shop with his father and hearing him addressed as 'boy'. In 1945 he contracted tuberculosis, and spent twenty months in a Sophiatown hospital. During this time of hospitalisation he was visited once a week by Trevor Huddleston, then priest in charge of this suburb of Johannesburg. Trevor Huddleston became a source of inspiration for Tutu from this time onwards; in later years Desmond Tutu was to name his own son after him, and the two men have remained firm friends.

In 1950, having successfully recovered from TB, he completed his studies and went on to a teacher training college in Pretoria. From 1953 to 1957 he taught in Johannesburg and Krugersdorp, marrying Leah, a former pupil of his father, in those years. His life as a teacher came to an end when Dr Verwoerd introduced the 'Bantu Education Act', which enforced a discriminatory system of education; Desmond Tutu decided he could 'have no truck with it', and subsequently decided to enter the ministry of the Anglican Church in South Africa. He became a deacon in 1960, the year of Sharpeville, and after working in the Benoni district of Johannesburg was ordained in 1961. Moving to Britain the following year, he studied theology at King's College London, and also worked in the parish of St Albans and took up a post with the WCC. He returned to South Africa in 1967 and worked in the diocese of Grahamstown, and from 1970 to 1974 was a lecturer at the University of Botswana, Lesotho and Swaziland. He then spent another year in Britain, working in the diocese of Southwark.

It was after his return to South Africa in 1975 that his presence made itself increasingly felt in his own land. Appointed to increasingly influential positions—Dean of Johannesburg, Bishop of Lesotho, General Secretary of the South African Council of Churches—the courage and clarity of his responses to the apartheid system brought him recognition as a spokesman for the black majority in South Africa, whose political leaders were exiled or imprisoned. He drew on the Book of Exodus as an allegory of the black South African's situation, and steered the SACC on a steady course in the teeth of State opposition. In 1979 the South African government withdrew his passport after he had called on Denmark to boycott sales of South African coal; this confiscation was condemned in a statement signed by the Archbishop of Canterbury and twenty-four Bishops, which read in part: 'In our view no satisfactory reason has been given, and since Bishop Tutu has been charged with no crime, the confiscation of his passport must be seen as a seriously disturbing harassment of the SACC. This we deplore, and earnestly request that the Bishop's passport be returned to enable him to continue his ecumenical work.'

In May 1980 Bishop Tutu took part in a march in Johannesburg to protest against the arrest of Revd John Thorne, the former General Secretary of the SACC. The entire contingent of marchers (including thirty-five clergymen) were arrested, finger-printed, photographed and kept in the cells of the notorious police station in John Vorster Square. In the morning, after a court appearance, the marchers were released, and later fined R.50 each. Though Bishop Tutu commented later that the actions of the authorities—'they don't know how to react to peaceful demonstrations'—gave this incident more attention than it was perhaps worthy of, he said that it established an important point: 'No longer are we to be Churches that merely pass pious resolutions'.

Bishop Tutu's passport was eventually returned to him in January 1981, and shortly after that he left South Africa to visit Europe and the USA. He was in London in March 1981 when press reports came through indicating that the South African government, angered by his comments on the tour—that the South African regime was the most evil since the Nazis—intended to withdraw his passport again when he returned to South Africa. A press conference was called at the Headquarters of the British Council of Churches at which Bishop Tutu gave his reaction to this latest government action against him. He was unrepentant: he was after all talking about peaceful change, and this attempt to muzzle him should make the world community realise the kind of obstacles encountered when trying to talk to those whose sole interest was in holding on to their power and privileges.

It was not a solemn occasion, but there was an intensity too, revealed when he was asked about his attitude to the insurgents in South Africa. 'I would like to throw this question back to the West' he insisted—how could people praise the French resistance, or regard Dietrich Bonhoeffer as a hero for his involvement in the plot on Hitler's life and suddenly turn pacifist when blacks took up arms? Many of those fighting had been committed Christians, taking up the armed struggle as a last resort. Had not the Afrikaners, the USA and Britain all fought for their freedom?

While Tutu is working for a peaceful solution to South Africa's political problems, he feels bound to make the West aware that those who take up arms against the apartheid system have widespread support amongst the black population. 'The guerrillas are our children, our brothers and our sisters' he was quoted as saying in the British press. The West should not see them in the same light as the Baader-Meinhof group or the Red Brigade because 'in their countries there are political institutions available to those who take up the gun. In South Africa there are none.'

However, the Anglican Church and its Archbishop continue to hope that reason will prevail, and that the government will release the imprisoned black leaders and negotiate a political solution to South Africa's problems. As the 1980s came to an end there were signs that this course was becoming easier for the white population to contemplate, for it was at this point that the new leader of the ruling Nationalist Party, F. W. de Klerk, made some important and unprecedented concessions. Walter Sisulu, the ANC leader and colleague of Nelson Mandela, was released and held press conferences and mass meetings under the ANC banner, events previously unthinkable in South Africa. Under de Klerk's leadership the segregation of beaches has been ended, and criticisms of police brutality have been openly aired, as well as allegations about South African assassination squads abroad. The demonising of the African National Congress was made to look fanciful by Walter Sisulu's demeanour, and the discipline he brought to his followers helped to bring a new atmosphere to South Africa's political life. His release paved the way for the momentous release of Nelson Mandela in February 1990, which has brought rejoicing to the black South African community, and has been a further step in the right direction.

A clue about the direction the white population could take in future years is found in one of the speeches in this collection. Tutu says he looks forward to a South Africa 'which will be a launching pad not just for Southern Africa but for the whole of the continent, to propel it into the twenty-first century and beyond'. The vision is of a free South Africa which would no longer drain Africa of resources and vitality, but would be able to help the continent to overcome its myriad problems. By contributing to Africa the white South African would finally find an identity in Africa, founded not on force or fear, but on respect.

When one thinks of the role the Church has not infrequently played in society in the past—a role that has led to excesses such as the Crusades or the Inquisition—it is good to see a section of the Church openly identifying with the poor and oppressed, and willing to speak up for those without a voice. In Tutu's work one feels that the Church is returning to the core of Christianity—both applying Christ's ethical principles in a situation of great tension, and attempting to create a space in society and people's hearts for the spirit of Christ the peacemaker and reconciler. In his love of life and his awareness of human potential he is moving on from the cheerless view of humanity that has done Christianity such a disservice in the past. Both in social and psychological terms Tutu's witness in South Africa has important lessons for the global Church, and his insights into South Africa are often relevant to global issues.

Perhaps he catches the spirit of the Church of the future; he certainly gives hope to people and communicates the feeling of the oppressed to the powerful, believing that peace and reconciliation are made more possible through this open, honest communication. Through his work we see a Church that has been weaned from its damaging complicity with the powerful, working for peace and justice and equality, and making a real and welcome contribution to our world.

JOHN WEBSTER
February 1990

SOUTHERN AFRICA

PART ONE

The Emerging Church

Part One summarises the theological basis for Archbishop Tutu's public work, and his belief that the spiritual beliefs of the Christian have inescapable social implications—in his own words, that 'Christianity can never be a merely personal matter'.

The Emerging Church

1. Jesus Christ—the man for others

Taken from sermons preached by Bishop Tutu in the Cathedrals of Johannesburg, Maritzburg and New York.

THE GOD whom we worship is wonderfully transcendent—St John in his Gospel sums it all up by saying 'God is Spirit'. Yet when this God wanted to intervene decisively in the affairs of Man, he did not come as a spiritual being. He did not come as an angel. No, he became a human being. He came in a really human and physical way—his mother became pregnant, and he was born as a helpless baby, depending on mother and father for protection, for food, for love and for teaching. When they looked for him in the houses of Kings and the high and mighty, he was born in a stable, as one of the lowly and despised. He worked as the village carpenter, knowing what it meant for a mother to lose her only coin, to sweep out the house diligently by candlelight, until she found the lost coin and rejoiced at the finding.

If we could go back to the days when our Lord walked here on earth and we asked people: 'What sort of person is this Jesus?' we would get many different answers. Some would say 'Oh, he tells such beautiful but funny stories—he really is a powerful creature'. Or, 'He is very brave—he is not afraid of the rulers'. But I am sure most people would say: 'Really, I have never seen anyone who cares so much for people, especially people in trouble. He cared for us when we were in the wilderness and we were hungry. God gave him the power to multiply the bread and fishes and he fed us. His disciples had said he should send us away hungry and he had refused.' Nowhere are we told that he ever turned anybody away who was in need; no matter how busy he was he never neglected anybody.

There is nothing that might be called otherworldly about this ministry of Jesus. He scandalised the religious leaders of his day, the prim and proper ones, because he consorted with the social and religious pariahs of his day. The religious establishment saw him as a young upstart who had no religious training, who had not sat at the feet of any renowned rabbi. What was more, he came to

3

turn upside down everything they knew. He came sowing all kinds of confusion. He had dared to have dinner with Zaccheus, a tax collector, a collaborator with the Roman oppressor, and had had the temerity to call him the son of Abraham. He had invited another tax collector, Levi, to become one of his special followers. He had gone to dinner in his house, and there, quite horribly, incredibly, he had sat at the table with all the riff-raff of the town, those whom every respectable person would not be seen dead with, let alone supping with them—those prostitutes, those sinners, those drug addicts, the so-called scum of society. Moreover, when the establishment men, the Pharisees and the Sadducees, those who knew everything about God and religion, when they challenged him, he was not in the least embarrassed. No, he said: 'Only the sick need a doctor, not those who are well'. He said he had come to find those who were lost. He even said, quite unbelievably, that these prostitutes, these sinners, would precede the religious teachers and leaders into Heaven. Jesus revolutionised religion by showing that God was really a disreputable God, a God on the side of the social pariahs. He showed God as one who accepted us sinners unconditionally.

We could not accuse our Lord of using religion as a form of escapism from the harsh realities of life, as most people live and experience it. The jibe of the Marxist could not apply to him—he never used religion as an opiate of the people, promising them 'pie in the sky when you die'. He knew that people want their pie here and now, and not in some future tomorrow. A postmortem pie is an oddity in any case. No, for he described in the parable of the last judgement what makes us fit or unfit for Heaven, and those criteria have nothing that you could call religious or otherwordly, in the narrow sense, about them. We qualify ourselves for Heaven by whether we have fed the hungry, clothed the naked, visited the sick or those imprisoned. And Jesus said to do these things to the least of his brethren, is to have done them as to him.

We need to remind ourselves constantly that Jesus was heir to the prophetic tradition. You cannot read any of the major prophets without being struck by at least one thing. They all condemned, as worthless religiosity, a concern with offering God worship when we were unmindful of the socio-political implica-

4

tions of our religion. Such worship and religion they condemned roundly as quite unacceptable to God, and for that reason an abomination and worthless. For Jesus, as for them, all of life belongs as a whole to God, both in its secular and sacred aspects. They could not have understood our peculiar habit of compartmentalising life, and nor could Jesus.

Listen to Isaiah 58.1–8; the same words can be echoed by other prophets.

The Lord says, 'Shout as loud as you can! Tell my people Israel about their sins! They worship me every day, claiming that they are eager to know my ways, and obey my laws. They say that they want me to give them just laws, and that they take pleasure in worshipping me.'

The people ask, 'Why should we fast if the Lord never notices? Why should we go without food if he pays no attention?'

The Lord says to them, 'The truth is that at the same time as you fast, you pursue your own interests and oppress your workers. Your fasting makes you violent, and you quarrel and fight. Do you think this kind of fasting will make me listen to your prayers? When you fast you make yourselves suffer; you bow your heads low like a blade of grass, and you spread out sackcloth and ashes to lie on. Is that what you call fasting? Do you think I will be pleased with that?

The kind of fasting I want is this: remove the chains of oppression, and the yoke of injustice, and let the oppressed go free. Share your food with the hungry, and open your homes to the homeless poor. Give clothes to those who have nothing to wear, and do not refuse to help your own relatives.

Then my favour will shine on you like the morning sun, and your wounds will be quickly healed. I will always be with you to save you; my presence will protect you on every side.'

Jesus believed that he was fighting against the evil one on behalf of God to establish God's Kingdom. Suffering, hunger, disease, poverty—all these things were the result of evil. He spoke of disease sometimes as bondage—Satan had enslaved the sick person, because he did not like us to be free. And Jesus came to bring wholeness and healing where there was disease.

An equally important truth about Jesus was that he was a man of prayer, a man of God. It was the intimate communion with his Father which formed his life's blood. Thus we can understand his cry of dereliction and anguish, 'My God, My God, why hast thou forsaken me?', when our sins blotted out for him his experience of God the Father. Prayer, and communion with the Father were like breathing to him. We see him going into a forty-day retreat, to learn about the nature of his vocation as a Messiah. Prayer and spirituality were central in the life of our Lord, and he was the man for others only because first and foremost he had been the man of God.

2. The Church in the world

Taken from an address given in Pretoria at the Presbyterian Church Assembly, and from a sermon preached at St Cyprian's Church in Sharpeville.

THIS TWOFOLD movement or pattern in our Lord's life must be ours as well. We cannot use religion as a form of escapism, skulking behind our prayers, because that cannot be an authentic Christian spirituality. Equally we cannot engage in a merely worldly 'busyness' or activism. For then what do we bring that is distinctive to the hectic business of sorting out our problems?

The Church of God has to be the salt and light of the world. We are the hope of the hopeless, through the power of God. We must transfigure a situation of hate and suspicion, of brokenness and separation, of fear and bitterness. We have no option. We are servants of the God who reigns and cares. He wants us to be the alternative society; where there is harshness and insensitivity, we must be compassionate and caring; where people are statistics, we must show they count as being of immense value to God; where there is grasping and selfishness, we must be a sharing community now.

In the early Church people were attracted to it not so much by the preaching, but by the fact that they saw Christians as a community, living a new life as if what God had done was important, and had made a difference. They saw a community of those who, whether poor or rich, male or female, free or slave, young or old—all quite unbelievably loved and cared for each other. It was the lifestyle of the Christians that was witnessing.

We witness too, by being a community of reconciliation, a forgiving community of the forgiven. We need it in the world today, don't we? But how can we say we offer the remedy to the world's hatreds and divisions, if we ourselves as Christians are divided into different churches, if we are unforgiving, if we don't greet or speak to certain people? People will be right to say 'Physician heal thyself!' We must not only speak about forgiveness and reconciliation—we must act on these principles.

We must witness by service to others, by being their servants in all sorts of ways. In our country, South Africa, the Church must be there in the poverty and squalor, to bring the love and compassion of God amongst the sick, the hungry, the lepers, the disabled and the naked. We must proclaim that in a country of injustice and oppression, where blacks receive an inferior education, are forced to live in matchbox houses, cannot move freely from place to place, and have to leave their wives and families behind when they want to work in town—we must declare that this is God's world. He is on the side of the oppressed, of the poor, of the despised ones. We must say these things even if they make us suffer. It is not politics. It is the Gospel of Jesus Christ the liberator who will set us free. In this country those who say these things are detained without trial, as your new rector was. They are banned, they are threatened with death, as your Minister was. But we cannot keep quiet, because if we kept quiet then the very stones would cry out. When they knew Bishop Tutu was coming to preach here today [*at St Cyprian's, Sharpeville*] then the Special Branch came. You saw them as we were processing around the township—sitting in their

7

cars to watch the Church of God. Let us be the Church of God, fearlessly proclaiming his Gospel.

The identification with the poor is a costly business. It leads to vilification and ostracism. Christ not only suffered but was eventually killed for it. If the Church is a serving Church, it will be a suffering Church as well. Suffering is a hard fact of reality, and human beings have, down the ages, tried to make sense of what appeared to be so meaningless. The dualists claimed there were two eternal principles: a God of goodness, light and spirit, who was in conflict with a God of evil, darkness and matter. Suffering occurred because our world was the arena for this conflict.

The Hindu or Buddhist deal with suffering by saying it doesn't really exist—it is all illusion. Unfortunately someone with an excruciating toothache does not find much relief in being told it is illusory. Another view that has been influential down the ages is the one that says: 'You suffer because you are a sinner'. However, Jesus repudiated this view: when confronted with a man born blind and asked whether he or his parents had sinned, he responded that neither had sinned.

The breakthrough in Biblical teaching came when suffering could be seen as redemptive, and not merely wasteful. This teaching was fulfilled in Jesus Christ. He suffered and died for us, overcoming suffering and making available to us the same power. While on earth he did all he could to alleviate want, pain and anguish, yet he knew he had to suffer. It is of the essence of Christianity, because he said, 'Unless you take up your cross and follow me, you cannot be my disciple'. An affluent, comfortable Church cannot be the Church of Christ—an affluent Church which uses its wealth for itself.

We must do all we can to alleviate suffering; there is so much to be done in this South Africa of plenty and affluence, where there is malnutrition, families sleeping on pavements, after being evicted from a house that stands empty behind them, just because they are the wrong colour. But having done all, there will still be suffering which remains for us a mystery. We know that our God is not an aloof, unmoved God. He came into our human existence, he knows it from inside and is touched by our anguish.

8

3. Politics and religion

From an article in Kairos, *the journal of the South African Council of Churches, 23 October 1978.*

IT IS interesting that when a religious leader should support a particular political system he is hardly ever accused of dabbling in politics. But woe betide the religious leader when he has the temerity to criticise a particular political status quo. He then runs the gauntlet of harsh criticism—for being a political predikant. For us it is not politics that determines our attitudes and actions. It is quite firmly our Christian faith which determines our socio-political involvement. We ask: is such and such an action, policy or attitude consonant with our understanding of the teachings of Jesus Christ? How does it square up to what he called the summary of the Law—loving God and loving one's neighbour; the two sides of the same coin.

So the Christian must always be critical of all political systems, always testing them against Gospel standards. Does this system usurp the place of God? Does the State require an absolute loyalty, a loyalty that deifies it? The State should be obeyed when it remains in its legitimate authority, but there are circumstances when it forfeits the allegiance of its subjects. The Christian's ultimate loyalty and obedience are to God, not to a movement or a cause, or a political system. If certain laws are not in line with the imperatives of the Gospel then the Christian must agitate for their repeal by all peaceful means.

Christianity can never be a merely personal matter. It has public consequences and we must make public choices. Many people think Christians should be neutral, or that the Church must be neutral. But in a situation of injustice and oppression such as we have in South Africa, not to choose to oppose, is in fact to have chosen to side with the powerful, with the exploiter, with the oppressor.

4. Reflections on Liberation theology

IN THE recent past, it used to be taken for granted that when you talked about Christian theology, then you were really referring to theology as it had been done or was being done in the great centres of Christianity in Western Christendom. You would be thought to be discussing theology as it was being written, taught or discussed in the UK, North America or on the European Continent, especially in Germany. If you came from a Third World country, you would be expected to study the theologians produced in these great centres, if you yourself aspired to be a theologian who wanted to be taken account of in the future!

But we note that some of the best theologies have come not from the undisturbed peace of a don's study, or his speculations in a university seminar, but from a situation where they have been hammered out on the anvil of adversity, in the heat of battle, or soon thereafter. For too long Western theology has wanted to lay claim to a universality that it cannot too easily call its own. Christians have found that the answers they possessed, were answers to questions that nobody in different situations was asking. New theologies have arisen, addressing themselves to the issues in front of them. Consequently we have in our midst now the theology of Liberation, as developed in Latin America, and Black theology, developed in the USA and Southern Africa.

The perplexity they have to deal with is this: Why does suffering single out black people so conspicuously, suffering not at the hands of pagans or other unbelievers, but at the hands of white fellow Christians who claim allegiance to the same Lord and Master?

A few years ago it became fashionable to say that the world sets the agenda for the Church. This represented a salutary shift of emphasis away from our unhealthy otherworldliness. Christians had wanted to shut themselves in a holy ghetto, almost entirely unmindful of the cries of the hungry, and the anguish of the poor and exploited ones of this world. There was an almost Manichean dread of the material, existent world, and Christians had to deny in an absolute way the world, the flesh and the devil—in order to

10

concentrate on the world to come. Those who reacted against this unsatisfactory state of affairs declaimed approvingly that 'God loved not the Church, but the world'. Such a reminder was important; it represented a positive gain and we must give thanks that it happened. And yet one has the suspicion that the pendulum of reaction might just have swung too far, and that (to change the image) the baby has been thrown out with the bath water. What I am trying to underline is that we cannot denigrate the Church, and devalue it, because we want to enhance the value of the world.

In South Africa, to refer now to some specifics, the Church of God must sustain the hope of a people who have been tempted to grow despondent, because the powers of this world seem to be rampant. It does not appear that significant political change can happen without much bloodshed and violence, and it seems that God does not care, or is impotent. The Church of God must say that despite all appearances to the contrary, this is God's world. He cares and cares enormously, his is ultimately a moral universe that we inhabit, and that right and wrong matter, and that the resurrection of Jesus Christ proclaims that right will prevail. Goodness and Love, Justice and Peace are not illusory, or mirages that forever elude our grasp. We must say that Jesus Christ has inaugurated the Kingdom of God, which is a Kingdom of Justice, Peace and Love, or fullness of life, that God is on the side of the oppressed, the marginalised and the exploited. He is a God of the poor, of the hungry, of the naked, with whom the Church identifies and has solidarity. The Church in South Africa must be the prophetic Church, which cries out 'Thus saith the Lord', speaking up against injustice and violence, against oppression and exploitation, against all that dehumanises God's children and makes them less than what God intended them to be.

PART TWO

The Struggle for Justice in South Africa

The following section reveals how Bishop Tutu, as leader of the South African Council of Churches, took on the apartheid regime and appealed to the general public, to students, to the country's broadcasters and finally to the government for fundamental political change in the country. It was this that brought the SACC into the firing line, but when attacked by government ministers he defended himself and the organisation he headed 'in strong terms'. His work with the SACC brought him to world attention, and was a major factor in the award of the Nobel Peace Prize.

PART TWO

The struggle for purity in South Africa

5. Crisis and response

From an article entitled 'South Africa in crisis and our response as the children of God'.

THE SOUTH AFRICAN Council of Churches (SACC) has issued serious warnings that unless fundamental change occurs in the Republic reasonably quickly, then those who are working for peaceful change will rapidly become discredited. Many people, in desperation, will want to use violence as a last desperate resort. At this stage we in the SACC are still striving for a peaceful solution of the crisis in our land. But time is not on our side. Something must be done, and done urgently.

But a time of crisis is not just a time of anxiety and worry. It gives a chance, an opportunity, to choose well or to choose badly. You have to decide which way you want to go. It is possible in our country to choose the path that leads to a new and more open society—a society that is more just, where people matter because they were created in the image of God. Equally it is possible to choose the road that leads to our destruction, because it is the road of injustice and oppression. And we believe that unless we have real change in this beloved land, then we are going to have a bloodbath.

We want to avert that awful alternative. We in the SACC are committed to work for justice and peace! We are committed to reconciliation. We believe that the Churches can demonstrate the kind of society we are working for—a caring and compassionate society, where you count because you are a human being, and not because of your colour or your race. Some of this is already happening in a few of our churches. In St Mary's Cathedral in Johannesburg, black and white worship together under the leadership of a black Dean. In the SACC we have a staff of all races, black, white and brown, and all work harmoniously together. It can happen in the whole of South Africa. Please let us move away from the edge of the precipice. God is giving us perhaps our last chance.

15

6. The South African problem and black protest

From an address given at the University of Witwatersrand.

THE PROBLEM in South Africa is to do with political power as between white and black. When the Afrikaners came to power in 1948 they created laws, or reinforced others, which increased the total unacceptability for blacks of white minority rule. Nobody, or relatively few amongst the whites, are as opposed to white minority rule, as they are to so-called black majority rule. I believe in majority rule, not *black* majority rule. That is what democracy is about, and dear vilified former terrorist Mugabe, now Prime Minister *Mr* Mugabe, has shown what blacks can do, and how magnanimous they are. He is no racist.

Blacks execrated, and still execrate with their whole beings the system of white minority rule. They are pledged to see it changed or destroyed. They have protested since the beginning of this century, against the gross injustices and inequities they have experienced. They have gone on delegations overseas; they have waited on governments in South Africa; they have signed petitions; they have staged protest marches; they have appealed for justice and fairness, and for the removal of structural violence. They have protested against low pay and the pass laws, they have participated in puppet impotent bodies set up by the government, in the hope that their willingness to co-operate would demonstrate their earnestness to the government, and thus elicit greater understanding of their plight. It has all, it appears, been in vain. The best organised and most widespread protest in which blacks participated, was the passive resistance campaign of the 1950s, when black people deliberately broke immoral and discriminatory laws. In many ways this led to the protests against the Pass Laws, which culminated in the Sharpeville killings of 21 March 1960. The world was appalled that blacks, protesting peacefully, could be mowed down so ruthlessly; many were shot in the back, and there was never any question of the police being in danger.

That is part of our history, etched forever into our memories, and burning itself into black psyches. Following the pattern shown in the Afrikaner resistance movement [*against the British*], there has been an escalation in the black protest movement. There has been a disengagement following the failure of appeals and verbal protests. We have seen the disengagement from white contact through the Black Consciousness movement—a movement absolutely crucial to true reconciliation.

And so we came to the Soweto riots of June 1976. Afrikaners, who had fought against English being imposed on them, in their turn wanted to impose Afrikaans upon the blacks, who rightly or wrongly, regard it as the language of the oppressor. There was an explosion South Africa had not been prepared for, not even the police, who had riddled our society with despicable creatures called informers. After 16 June 1976 our white fellow South Africans were frightened. They thought Armageddon had arrived. Gun shops were emptied of their stock.

Afrikaans was a symbol of a whole system of oppression, injustice and exploitation. Cheap labour, the destruction of black family life, overcrowded trains and buses, small matchbox houses in dreary smog-filled townships (which lack the most elementary amenities which other sections of the community take for granted), a system of education deliberately inferior to that of the other communities—all these and more were symbolised by the Afrikaans issue. So South Africa went up in flames.

But even now nothing much has changed. Black anger is growing. Blacks are being endorsed out even more stringently, and dumped anywhere, as long as they are out of sight and so out of mind. They are starving in a country that boasts of sending food to Zambia, to starve as part of the solution of the South African political crisis, the so-called solution which is that there will be no black South Africans.

Thus many blacks have said: 'We give up. We have tried everything peaceful and we have failed. Our last resort is to fight for the right to be human, for the right to be a South African.' And so South Africa faces the prospect of a civil war again. The Voortrekkers protested, then disengaged, then fought. Blacks have protested, have disengaged, and some of them are now fighting. Whites have boys on the border; blacks have boys on the other side.

17

What we say is: there is probably just time for a reasonably peaceful resolution of our crisis. We are still crying out that we are committed to justice, reconciliation and peace. We are still holding out our hands of fellowship, and saying to our white compatriots 'grasp them—let us talk while there is still time. If we can solve our crisis then we have as South Africans, black and white together, a tremendous contribution to make to Africa and the rest of the world. God has blessed us with a wonderful country, large enough to accommodate and support all of us, black and white, most comfortably.'

If the government however, is determined to balkanise South Africa, and snatch away citizenship from blacks, then there will not be a peaceful solution, for they are declaring war on us. What are blacks then expected to do in such a situation? Fold their hands?

7. Challenge and invitation to white students

While an increasing number of students are becoming involved in the struggle for social change, many are still content to accept their unjust privileges. This challenge to them, with the preceding analysis of the South African situation, was delivered to an audience of students at Witwatersrand University, on 18 March 1980, at a meeting of the Student Representative Council's Academic Freedom Committee.

Is THIS present South Africa what you want for your children, a divided segregated South Africa where there is freedom for no one really? *You* suffer also because of discrimination, you are diminished because you can't have as a neighbour anyone you want. Your choices are limited—you have to marry into certain races which are determined for you. You can't discuss openly and freely. What do you really know about Communism or Marxism?

You are brainwashed by the South African Broadcasting Corporation (SABC) which constantly misleads you, as it does its propaganda work for the Nationalist party. And you just sit around and do nothing about it.

In your name various people are banned, even after fifteen years on Robben Island. They come out of prison, where they could hardly be said to have engaged in subversive activities, only to be banned for another five years, to be prisoners at their own expense. You sit around and do nothing about it, you say nothing about it. You are too busy getting your degrees, so that you can be qualified to enter the rat-race. But all these actions are done in your name, and in the name of Christian civilisation and free enterprise. In your name people are locked up in detention barracks because they are opposed to all wars as pacifists. You accept it all quite comfortably. You sleep in your white sheets after a sumptuous meal, and you say and do nothing about a government which refuses people the right of conscientious objection. South Africa is the only country in the so-called free world which denies the right of conscientious objection. A priest is given a vicious sentence for attending a Church conference and you say and do nothing about it. Blacks are moved like so many cattle from place to place, to preserve your identity and your privilege, and you go on as if nothing untoward had occurred. *All these diabolical schemes occur in your name.* Even after the Sharpeville massacre, the Soweto riots, you seem quite content to have it so, for you say and do virtually nothing.

We are committed to black liberation, because thereby we are committed to white liberation. You will never be free until we blacks are free. So join the liberation struggle. Throw off your lethargy, and the apathy of affluence. Work for a better South Africa for ourselves, and for our children. Uproot all evil and oppression and injustice of which blacks are victims and you whites are beneficiaries, so that you won't reap the whirlwind. Join the winning side. Oppression, injustice, exploitation—all these have lost, for God is on 'our side' on the side of justice, of peace, of reconciliation, of laughter and joy, of sharing and compassion and goodness and righteousness.

St Paul asks, 'If God be for us, who can be against us?'

8. To the white South African community

The following two appeals, to South African whites and the media, are taken from an address entitled 'Change or Illusion', delivered at a Black Sash Conference, on 10 March 1980.

Percy Qoboza was the former editor of The World, *South Africa's leading black newspaper, which was banned by the government. Dr Motlana is a Soweto civic leader.*

TO THE white community in general I say—express your commitment to change, by agreeing to accept a redistribution of wealth, and a more equitable sharing of the resources of our land. Be willing to accept voluntarily a declension in your very high standard of living. Isn't it better to lose something voluntarily, and to assist in bringing about change—political powersharing—in an orderly fashion, rather than seeing this come about through bloodshed and chaos, when you will stand to lose everything? Change your attitudes. Realise that blacks are human beings, and all we want is to be treated as such. Everything you want for yourselves is exactly what we want for ourselves and for our children—a stable family life where husband lives with wife and children, adequate housing, and proper free and compulsory education for our children.

All the current black political leaders, who are acknowledged as such by the black community, are ready to talk. It is no good engaging in a charade with leaders whom most blacks repudiate. Look at what happened to Bishop Muzorewa. Our real leaders are eminently reasonable, and I include those on Robben Island and in exile. Percy Qoboza pointed out that these were the last generation that will be ready to negotiate. Please let us talk while we can, whilst there is a real possibility of an orderly evolution to a shared society. I have dedicated myself to help bring this about, yet when you hear references to people such as Dr Motlana or Percy Qoboza or myself, you could be forgiven for thinking that we were firespouting radical Marxists who were touting Russian-made guns.

9. To the South African Broadcasting Corporation

I HAVE not given up hope for the SABC, as a heaven-sent opportunity to help change attitudes in South Africa, and to help pave the way for change. If the SABC stopped being a propaganda machine, it could begin to educate whites for change. Its interviewers would not be such supine obsequious people, bowing and scraping when they are talking to someone in authority, and being abrasive to the point of rudeness with critics of the horrendous system. I hear that the SABC went to town about the remarks of a certain magistrate, and of Bishop Mokoena regarding my character. They did not think to hear my side, because, as Percy Qoboza has said, the SABC are past masters at character assassination, and are hard put to it to recognise truth—even when it stares them in the face. I urge the SABC to have a passion for truth, and leave propaganda to the party political machines. People are sacked for showing what Baragwanath hospital is really like, or even Soweto. 'What is unseen does not exist, and to ignore something long enough means it will disappear'—that seems to be the motto of the SABC. You must change, and so help South Africa prepare for change.

In October 1989, ten years after this piece was written, Desmond Tutu at last began to appear on SABC television.

21

10. The South African Council of Churches—our work at the grassroots

The remainder of this Part looks at some aspects of the SACC's work: its work for human rights, the way that the Nationalist government reacted to the SACC's political involvement, and the way that Bishop Tutu defended the Council. Clearly relations between the SACC and the government were at an all-time low in October 1979.

WE IN the SACC believe in a non-racial South Africa, where people count because they are made in the image of God. So the SACC is neither a black nor a white organisation. It is a Christian organisation with a definite bias in favour of the oppressed and the exploited ones of our society. In a small way we in the SACC offices are the first fruits of this new South Africa. We have nearly all the races of South Africa, belonging to most of the major denominations, working together as a team, headed by a General Secretary who happens to be black. The sun, so far as I can make out, still rises in the East and sets in the West, and I have not noticed that the sky has fallen because whites might have to take instructions from blacks. They are not blacks or whites. No, they are Wolfram, Thom, Anne, Margaret, Father Tutu.

The gospel of Jesus Christ teaches us that true power lies not with the powerful, but with the powerless for whom he specially cared. We are challenged by our Lord's example to work for those in prison, the poor and oppressed, the homeless and despised. The Dependants Conference (DC) is a division of the SACC—it serves banned persons, detainees, political prisoners and their families. It is responsible for the welfare of all such people when, by reason of having been imprisoned or banned, they are deprived of adequate means of support. The Dependants Conference is currently looking after 700 families of political prisoners, and has a budget of about R.700,000 per annum (1979 figures). DC arranges for relatives to visit their folk on Robben Island. You can imagine what a visit from a wife, or other relative, must mean to someone sentenced to a minimum of five years—or even life imprisonment.

Through the generosity of the diocese of Cape Town, DC has been able to rent a hostel to accommodate these visitors, who come from all over the country and Namibia. They can usually fit in two visits during their stay—two visits for the whole year.

Jesus said, when I was in prison you visited me—that is our mandate for this work. DC also tries to enable released political prisoners to get back to a normal life, by providing means of self-support or finding employment. We helped a man who had seven children. He died and we continued to help his family. Then the widow died, and DC is now the only source of sustenance for the seven orphaned children. Strangely enough, it is for work such as this—when we try to obey our Lord—that the SACC is in bad odour.

The Asingeni Fund came into existence in June 1976 to provide relief, and help with funeral expenses for families affected by the uprisings of that year. Most of the funds have been used to provide legal aid. We do not necessarily support the accused, or condone their alleged crimes, but believe firmly in the principle that each person is entitled to the best legal defence possible. We are assisting in the proper administration of justice, and deserve to be commended rather than to be vilified. We have had some significant statistics. In the cases where we have provided legal assistance we have notched up an acquittal rate of between 70% to 75%. Where people have been undefended, the conviction rate has been as high as 80%. Recently, through legal services that the SACC provided, a man sentenced to twelve years on Robben Island was acquitted on appeal. One such case is justification enough for continuing this work.

Is it being emotional or melodramatic to say that it is becoming increasingly criminal to be a Christian in South Africa? Well, try employing a so-called illegal black (someone who does not possess a pass or permit to work in urban areas). You are told that it is better to increase the unemployment figures—to consign people to the scrap heap of discarded people in the resettlement camps. What is the Church of God doing about it? What are we doing about it all? I believe we should tell people who are banned to ignore their banning orders, and let us support them when there are consequences. I think the Churches should mount a massive campaign of support, through positive non co-operation with the implementation of immoral, unchristian and unjust laws. Perhaps I should say that Churches should first urge the government to lift all banning orders forthwith, and failing this to mount a campaign.

The SACC is not always merely negative and critical of the authorities. We often send congratulatory messages to the government—we have commended Mr Botha for his courage, and praised Dr Koornhof for his reprieve of Crossroads and Alexander Township.

However, that SACC could not by any stretch of the imagination be called the blue-eyed boy of the Nationalist government. Since 1978 we have been regularly attacked by Cabinet Ministers and lesser mortals. Mr Kruger, then Minister of Justice and Police did his bit in 1978. Mr Schlebusch, his successor, warned the SACC after its National Conference of 1979 spoke in favour of supporting those who felt called to disobey state laws at variance with the law of God. Later in 1979 Mr Le Grange, the new Minister for Prisons and Police, attacked the SACC quite viciously. The climax came in May 1980, when the Prime Minister himself accused the SACC of fomenting unrest in the country, using the funds it had received mainly from overseas. In September of 1979 I was called to a meeting with Mr Schlebusch and Dr Koornhof, where I was asked to retract my 'coal statement', made in Copenhagen [*see page 28*], and apologise for having made it. I refused to do either. My passport was confiscated in February 1980, almost certainly as a punishment for my Denmark episode.

Church leaders have usually come to our support, repudiating the slurs cast against us, but it has often seemed as if we were operating in a country behind the Iron Curtain. Apart from this attention from the government, we have come under fire from the sanctimonious 'Christian League of South Africa', an organisation exposed as a front for the discredited Information Department, and one that was still receiving government funding until the end of 1979. But every time an attack has been levelled by the government or others at the SACC we have replied in strong terms against the accusations.

11. In Defence of the SACC

What follows is the text of a press statement, released on 11 October 1979, after Mr Le Grange made his attack on the SACC.

MR LOUIS LE GRANGE is quoted in newspaper reports as having made serious allegations against the SACC. My response is based on these reports which we hope are an accurate reflection of what the Minister said.

If these reports are correct then I can only say that I am deeply shocked, shocked that someone holding such a responsible position could speak so irresponsibly, so tendentiously and so untruthfully. It is distressing to find him picking up where his predecessor left off—making statements which cunningly link up the SACC and the Churches with, for instance, the Communist Party, so that there will be guilt by association and innuendo.

I want to declare categorically that I believe apartheid to be evil and immoral, and therefore unchristian. No theologian I know of would be prepared to say that the apartheid system is consistent with the Gospel of Jesus Christ. If Mr Le Grange thinks that blacks are *not* exploited, repressed and denied their human rights and dignity, then I invite him to be black for just one day. He would then hear Mr Arrie Paulus saying he is like a baboon, and a senior police officer saying he is violent by nature. He would be aware that in the land of their birth, black people, who form 80% of the population, have 13% of the land, and the white minority of about 20% has 87% of the land. In this country a white child of eighteen years can vote, but a black person, be he a university professor or a bishop or whatever, has no franchise. A black doctor with the same qualifications as his white counterpart is paid less for the same job. Have any whites had their homes demolished, and then been told to move to an inhospitable area, where they must live in tents until they have built themselves new houses? This happened last week to the Batlokwa people. I doubt very much that the Minister would still be able to say that apartheid was not an unchristian and unjust system, where human rights are denied.

I am sorry he speaks of propaganda actions on the part of the Churches. Fortunately, the Churches have *not* been guilty of using R.64 million to sell an unsellable commodity. [*See note for 'Message to Journalists' in Part Three, chapter 27.*]

Our Conference resolution on obeying God rather than man was taken by a responsible Conference, made up not of fire eating so-called leftists, but of Church leaders and duly elected representatives. The SACC and the Churches reserve the right to condemn, if need be, any legislation which is abhorrent to the Christian conscience, and which represents an abrogation of the rule of law. Certainly detention without trial, and the arbitrary banning of people are in this category, and we do not apologise for being ever vigilant in this regard.

Is the Minister aware of what he is saying when he accuses the SACC and the Churches of the crimes of providing relief for political detainees, and for providing legal defence for those involved in political trials? If these are crimes then we openly and proudly plead guilty. We declare that everybody is entitled to the best defence possible. We should be praised rather than vilified for our part in ensuring that there is an equitable administration of justice.

The SACC has been critical of the role of foreign investment, but has nowhere yet advocated, cautiously or otherwise, an anti-investment policy.

It seems it is reprehensible to condemn an educational system which is grossly lop-sided, and to advocate a more equitable distribution of resources for the greater good of an undivided South Africa. We are accused of doing something quite evil in trying to alleviate the distress of unemployed people, by helping them produce income through self-help projects. The Minister says we are exploiting the unemployment situation. We want to say, as respectfully as possible, that the Minister is talking arrant nonsense, and we would hope he would apologise for all these groundless attacks, especially this one. The Minister is guilty of gross untruths (and he knows it) when he says we have channelled funds to resistance movements. Why does he not use the wide powers he has to prosecute us, if we have done what is obviously so illegal in South Africa?

26

We know the tactics of this government. They plan to take action against the SACC, and they wish to prepare the public for that action. We want to remind them of a few things. First of all, they must stop playing at being God. They are human beings who happen to be carrying out an unjust and oppressive policy with a whole range of draconian laws. But they are still just mere mortals. And we are tired of having threats levelled against us. Why don't they carry them out?

Secondly, we want to warn Mr Le Grange, and others who may be tempted to emulate him. The SACC is a Council of Churches, not a private organisation. The Church has been in existence for nearly 2,000 years. Tyrants and others have acted against Christians during those years. They have arrested them, they have killed them, they have proscribed the faith. Those tyrants belong now to the flotsam and jetsam of forgotten history—and the Church of God remains, an agent of justice, of peace, of love and reconciliation. If they take the SACC and the Churches on, let them just know they are taking on the Church of Jesus Christ.

12. Where I stand

'Given a background such as this', wrote Bishop Tutu in Kairos, *the journal of the SACC, 'it was quite incredible that a meeting should take place between Church leaders and the Prime Minister.' The meeting was fixed for 7 August 1980, and three days before it took place, Bishop Tutu stated his position, in the following address given at the Pretoria Press Club.*

RECENTLY, WHEN I was on a flight from Durban, one of the pretty airhostesses approached me to say: 'Excuse me, Sir, a group of passengers would like you please to autograph a book for them'. Well, I thought, there are some nice people about who show they have a good sense of values. They appreciate a good thing when they see it. I was trying to look suitably modest, when she went on to say, 'You are Bishop Muzorewa, aren't you?'

That was an interesting episode, which in some ways was a comment on our South African situation. Bishop Muzorewa was a great favourite of most of white South Africa. Nobody seems to have thought to use the usual bit about his bringing politics into religion. This would indicate that as long as the politics one brings in is in favour, then one is not guilty of being a political cleric. I suppose that if I was to get up and say what it is quite impossible for me to do: 'Apartheid is not too bad; it is a genuine attempt to find a solution to our intractable problems'—I would become the blue-eyed boy of the Establishment, and not a whisper would be heard of my being a political hothead. SABC TV, which last interviewed me in 1978, would probably fall over themselves to get me on the box, instead of parading people who are generally unacceptable to the black community, to refute this or that statement that I have made.

For many whites, I am regarded as an irresponsible, radical fire-eater, who should have been locked up long ago, banned or had something equally horrible happen to me. I receive some quite hair-raising letters and telephone calls. My main sadness is when my family become the target of these obscene and demented calls. Then I really get angry. I am thankful that my family support me fully, in what I believe to be God's calling to me at this time, and that as a family we know that there is some cost in being involved, as most blacks and some whites are, in the liberation struggle to make South Africa truly free for all her children, black and white. But even so, it is painful to see one's child trembling with rage and shock because she has answered one of these calls.

I don't say this to evoke sympathy, or to pretend that we are heroes. It is merely to describe one facet of the reality that is contemporary South Africa. I was quite taken aback by the hostility against me, after my remark in Denmark about purchases of South African coal. [*In September 1979, during an interview on Danish television, Bishop Tutu said he thought it 'rather disgraceful' that Denmark was supporting the apartheid system by buying South African coal (after gold the country's largest export). When the interviewer replied that such a boycott would mean that 'a*

lot of blacks are going to be unemployed' he replied: 'They would be unemployed and suffer temporarily. It would be a suffering with a purpose. We would not be doing what is happening now, where blacks are suffering and it seems to be a suffering that is going to go on and on and on.' His comments caused a furore in South Africa.]
It was as if I had said: 'Blacks go to the rampage and rape every white woman in sight'. I don't think I could have aroused greater animosity if I had in fact been guilty of that sort of incitement to racial hatred and violence. In fact what I said was an attempt to make a sober contribution to finding a solution to our South African problem, without using violence. People are quite happy to talk about so-called peaceful means of change, as long as you canvass methods that everybody knows will be ineffectual; for basically, most whites want change as long as things remain the same, as long as they can go on enjoying their privileges and their high standard of living. That is why we urge the international community to exert as much political, diplomatic and economic pressure on South Africa as possible, to persuade us to get to the conference table. I love South Africa too passionately to want to see her destroyed, and international pressure may just avert that. And so in the perception of most whites in South Africa I am an ogre—something they will use to frighten children into obedience. I am, so they say, really a politician trying hard to be a bishop, and I manage with consummate skill to hide my horns under my funny bishop's hat, and my tail tucked away under my trailing cape.

But in reality I have no political ambitions whatsoever. In this respect I am no Bishop Muzorewa, Archbishop Makarios or Ayatollah Khomeini. (Indeed these gentlemen could be said to provide three reasons why religious leaders should not be politicians in the party political sense.) As I have said, it is my Christian faith which constrains me to behave in the way that I do. For me, through my fallible understanding of the scriptures, apartheid can only be described as blasphemous, and therefore I cannot but oppose it with every fibre in my being, and try to do all that I can, nationally and internationally, to have it changed.

Some say I want to promote a confrontation with the state. Nothing could be further from the truth. I believe fervently that when the state does the things that are proper to it, then it commands obedience. But when it exceeds its bounds, when it wants to claim what belongs to God for itself, then it is a religious duty to condemn this abuse of power, for Jesus said 'Render unto Caesar the things that are Caesar's, and to God the things that are God's'. When the laws have been passed by the people, or through their democratically elected representatives, and when the laws are just, then they must be obeyed. But South Africa's laws fail to pass that stringent test. None of them have been passed by the people's democratically elected representatives, because 80% of the people are excluded from the democratic process of law-making, and many of the laws, the whole apartheid system, is patently unjust.

So apartheid is a system which is not only unjust, but totally immoral and totally unchristian. Its claim that God created us human beings for separation, for apartness, and for division, contradicts the Bible and the whole tradition of undivided Christendom. God has created us for fellowship, for community, for friendship with God, and with one another, so that we can live in harmony with the rest of creation as well. For my part, the day will never come when apartheid will be acceptable. It is an evil system and it is at variance with the gospel of Jesus Christ. That is why I oppose it and can never compromise with it—not for political reasons but because I am a Christian.

13. Bishop Tutu's testimony

The meeting between the SACC and the government came about after requests from the SACC for a meeting to discuss the continuing critical situation in South Africa. Any hopes that there would be positive results were soon to be dashed. In fact, following this meeting relations between the government and the SACC became even more confrontational.

In addition the government managed to make political capital out of it, while the SACC lost some credibility amongst some black

Christians. But while one might be justified as regarding it as an occasion when the SACC was out-manoeuvred by the government, this meeting stands out as a courageous act on the SACC's part, an attempt at reconciliation and bridge building.

Bishop Tutu's own attitude towards the meeting is that 'it was not a conversation—there was a very wide gulf between the two sides. But it was a good thing that we tried to sit side by side, instead of fighting each other.'

What follows is Bishop Tutu's statement to the government.

WE HAVE no political axes to grind, and I think that should be stressed. The same gospel of Jesus Christ, which compels us to reject apartheid as totally unchristian, is the very gospel that constrains us to work for justice, for peace and reconciliation. God has given us a mandate to be ministers of his reconciliation.

We thank God that you and your government have come to recognise that the destiny of the peoples of South Africa cannot be decided by one group alone. We want to urge you, yet again, to negotiate for orderly change, by calling a National Convention, where our common future can be mapped out by the acknowledged leaders of every section of the South African population. To this end we believe fervently that the political prisoners in jail, in detention, in exile, must be permitted to attend such a convention. After all, your predecessor Mr Vorster counselled Mr Ian Smith to release black political prisoners, and sit around a conference table with them to try and hammer out a solution for their country.

It was your government which tried out a scheme similar to this in the Turnhalle talks relating to Namibia. Why should this way of dealing with apparently intractable problems be one that is for export only?

We believe that there can be no real peace in our beloved land until there is fundamental change. General Malan has said that the crisis in South Africa is 20% military and 80% political. You yourself have courageously declared that whites must be ready to adapt or die. This adapting, or change, has to go to the heart of the matter—to the dismantling of apartheid. Please believe us when we say there is much goodwill left, although we have to add that time and patience are running out. Hatred, bitterness and anger are growing, and unless something is done to demonstrate your intentions to bring about fundamental change, leading to power sharing, then we are afraid that the so-called ghastly alternative will be upon us. We recognise that this kind of fundamental change cannot happen overnight, and so we suggest that only four things need be done to give real hope that this change is going to happen. We can assure you that if we go along this road, you will gain most of South Africa and the world, while losing some of your party dissidents. These are the four points:

(1) LET THE GOVERNMENT COMMIT THEMSELVES TO A COMMON CITIZEN-SHIP IN AN UNDIVIDED SOUTH AFRICA.
If this does not happen we will have to kiss goodbye to peaceful change.

(2) PLEASE ABOLISH THE PASS LAWS.
Nothing is more hateful in a hateful system for blacks than these laws. Let it be a phased process, because none of us want to have a chaotic country. But I wish God could give me the words that could describe the dramatic change that would occur in relationships in this country, if the real abolition of the Pass Laws were to happen.

(3) PLEASE STOP IMMEDIATELY ALL POPULATION REMOVALS AND THE UPROOTING OF PEOPLE.
It is in my view totally evil and has caused untold misery.

(4) SET UP A UNIFORM EDUCATIONAL SYSTEM.
We are glad to note that you have agreed to the calling up of a commission to look into this matter. We want to suggest, in relation to this, that all universities be declared open, and that the black universities be free to appoint blacks who have credibility in the black community. Otherwise we fear that the unrest in these institutions will remain endemic.

If these four things were done, as starters, then we would be the first to declare out loud: please give the government a chance, they seem in our view to have embarked on the course of real change. I

32

certainly would be one of the first to shout this out from the rooftops. For then, through that process, we would all have *real* security, not a security that depends on force for its upholding. What a wonderful country we can have when we all, black and white, walk out heads high to this glorious future together. Because we will have a non-racial society, a just society, where everyone, black and white, is a child of God, created in his image. And you sir, will go down in history as a truly great man.

If this does not happen now, urgently, then I fear we will have to say we have had it. But God is good, and God loves all of us, and God has filled this country with his Holy Spirit. Let us be open to that Holy Spirit and share our fears and anxieties. Thank you.

In the Prime Minister's closing address it became clear that the SACC had not managed to convince the government of the need for real change—political powersharing—in South Africa. 'I am prepared to lead my people on the road . . . to create new dispensations', he said, 'but I am not prepared to lead them on the road of a government of one man one vote.'

PART THREE

Windows into South Africa

Some of the realities of South African life and the atmosphere in the country are evoked by the pieces in Part Three. Bishop Tutu preaches at the funeral of Steve Biko, and at a memorial service for Robert Sobukwe, two modern South African heroes, and looks around him at some of the effects of apartheid.

14. Steve Biko—a tribute

The singularly brutal way in which Steve Biko met his death at the hands of the South African Security Police outraged and saddened people throughout the world. Detained in Port Elizabeth on 18 August 1977, under Section 6 of the Terrorism Act, he was taken in chains to Pretoria—a bumping, bruising journey of 600 miles—in the back of a police Landrover. He died, aged thirty-one, after being kept naked and manacled, in detention on 12 September, as a result of the beatings he received in custody.

Steve Biko, thinker and activist, was born in King William's Town on 18 December 1946. In the late 1960s he formed SASO, the South African Students Organisation, and organised and wrote—sometimes under the name Frank Talk—until he was banned in March 1973. He was especially concerned with the building up of pride and awareness amongst his people, by demonstrating the worth of African culture, and by careful analysis of the processes by which the white settlers had stripped the black population of their freedom. This was the Black Consciousness Movement, which found expression in the rapidly outlawed Black People's Convention. He is now regarded as the founder of this movement. He called on black ministers of religion to support the cause of Black Consciousness by restoring direction and meaning to the black person's understanding of God.

The following tribute is taken from Bishop Tutu's oration at his funeral in King William's Town, and from his address at the SACC Memorial Service for Steve Biko, held at St George's Cathedral, Cape Town.

WHEN WE heard the news 'Steve Biko is dead' we were struck numb with disbelief. No, it can't be true! No, it must be a horrible nightmare, and we will awake and find that really it is different—that Steve is alive even if it be in detention. But no, dear friends, he is dead and we are still numb with grief, and groan with anguish 'Oh God, where are you? Oh God, do you really care—how can you let this happen to us?'

It all seems such a senseless waste of a wonderfully gifted

person, struck down in the bloom of youth, a youthful bloom that some wanted to see blighted. What can be the purpose of such wanton destruction? God, do you really love us? What must we do which we have not done, what must we say which we have not said a thousand times over, oh, for so many years—that all we want is what belongs to all God's children, what belongs as an inalienable right—a place in the sun in our own beloved mother country. Oh God, how long can we go on? How long can we go on appealing for a more just ordering of society where we all, black and white together, count not because of some accident of birth or a biological irrelevance—where all of us black and white count because we are human persons, human persons created in your own image.

God called Steve Biko to be his servant in South Africa—to speak up on behalf of God, declaring what the will of this God must be in a situation such as ours, a situation of evil, injustice, oppression and exploitation. God called him to be the founder father of the Black Consciousness Movement against which we have had tirades and fulminations. It is a movement by which God, through Steve, sought to awaken in the black person a sense of his intrinsic value and worth as a child of God, not needing to apologise for his existential condition as a black person, calling on blacks to glorify and praise God that he had created them black. Steve, with his brilliant mind that always saw to the heart of things, realised that until blacks asserted their humanity and their personhood, there was not the remotest chance for reconciliation in South Africa. For true reconciliation is a deeply personal matter. It can happen only between persons who assert their own personhood, and who acknowledge and respect that of others. You don't get reconciled to your dog, do you? Steve knew and believed fervently that being pro-black was not the same thing as being anti-white. The Black Consciousness Movement is not a 'hate white movement', despite all you may have heard to the contrary. He had a far too profound respect for persons as persons, to want to deal with them under readymade, shopsoiled categories.

All who met him had this tremendous sense of a warm-hearted man, and as a notable acquaintance of his told me, a man who was utterly indestructible, of massive intellect and yet reticent; quite unshakeable in his commitment to principle and to radical change in South Africa by peaceful means; a man of real reconciliation, truly an instrument of God's peace, unshakeable in his commitment to the liberation of all South Africans, black and white, striving for a more just and more open South Africa.

Steve saw, more than most of us, how injustice and oppression can dehumanise and make us all, black and white, victim and perpetrator alike, less than what God intended us to be. Now it has always sounded like sloganeering when people have said 'Oppression dehumanises the oppressor as well as the oppressed'. But have we not had an unbelievably shocking example of this, if he has been quoted correctly, in Mr Kruger's heartless remark that Steve's death 'leaves him cold'? Of all human beings, he is the most to be pitied. What has happened to him as a human being when the death of a fellow human being can leave him cold? And I bid you pray for the rulers of this land, for the police—especially the Security Police and those in the prison service—that they may realise that they are human beings too. I bid you pray for whites in South Africa.

It is no cheap slogan to say that Black Consciousness seeks, as Steve saw, the liberation of both black and white. Black Consciousness, in being concerned for black liberation, was, and is utterly committed, equally, to white liberation.

It was a man who was saying these things, it was a man who inspired us to share these thoughts, it was a man who infused others to a like commitment to justice, love, peace, reconciliation—all in South Africa—it was such a man that death, a mysterious death, struck down last Monday. We mourn such a tragic and apparently meaningless wasteful loss, the death of a splendid leader, already at the height of his powers, while still so young.

Let us pray for Ntsiki and all of Steve's family in this death. We weep for our land which has suffered a grievous blow, we weep for ourselves and yet we know that Steve lived his life as one that was always being laid down for his friends and his enemies; so that his death, ghastly as it is, was a consummation of such a life—the greatest love a person can have for his friends is to lay down his life

39

for them. Steve knew other words which that other remarkable young man, Jesus, had uttered. 'In truth, in very truth, I tell you, a grain of wheat remains a solitary grain unless it falls into the ground and dies; but if it dies, it bears a rich harvest. The man who loves himself is lost, but he who hates himself in this world will be kept safe for eternal life. If anyone serves me, he must follow me; where I am, my servant will be. Whoever serves me will be honoured by my Father.' (John 12.24–26)

So you see, Steve has started something that is quite unstoppable. The powers of evil, of injustice, of oppression, of exploitation, have done their worst and they have lost. They have lost because they are immoral and wrong, and our God, the God of Exodus, the liberator God, is a God of justice and righteousness, and he is on the side of justice and liberation and goodness. Our cause, the cause of justice and liberation, must triumph because it is moral and just and right. Many who support the present unjust system in this country, know in their hearts that they are upholding a system that is evil and unjust and oppressive, and which is utterly abhorrent and displeasing to God. There is no doubt whatsoever that freedom is coming. (Yes, it may be a costly struggle still, but we are experiencing today the birth pangs of a new South Africa.) The darkest hour, they say, is before the dawn. We are experiencing the birth pangs of a new South Africa, a free South Africa, where all of us, black and white together, will walk tall, where all of us, black and white together, will hold hands as we stride forth on the Freedom March, to usher in the new South Africa. We thank and praise God for giving us such a magnificent gift in Steve Biko, and for his sake, and the sake of ourselves and our children, let us dedicate ourselves anew to the struggle for the liberation of our beloved land, South Africa.

15. Robert Mangaliso Sobukwe

Robert Sobukwe was born in 1924, in the Cape Province. He was active in the non-violent protest campaigns of the 1950s, losing his job as a teacher for taking part in the Defiance Campaign of 1952. In the late 1950s he was instrumental in setting up the Pan Africanist Congress (PAC), which broke away from the African National Congress (ANC) in 1959. He was elected its president, and resigned from his post of lecturer in African languages at the University of Witwatersrand to lead the anti-pass law protests in 1960. These protests were greeted with an infamous display of state violence: at Sharpeville, on 21 March 1960, the police opened fire on the unarmed crowd, killing 67 people, and wounding 186.

Robert Sobukwe was arrested and sentenced to three years' imprisonment, and on his release, was detained on Robben Island for six years, by a special Act of Parliament. Released in 1969, he was then banned, and confined to the district of Kimberley. Affectionately known as 'the Prof.', he died in 1978.

This tribute is the text of the address delivered by Bishop Tutu at the SACC memorial service, 6 March 1978.

LAST SEPTEMBER, I was privileged to take part in a memorial service in St George's Cathedral, Cape Town, for Steve Biko—that grand stalwart of Africa—little thinking that only a matter of six months later I would be participating in a memorial service for an even grander stalwart, a giant among men, Robert Mangaliso Sobukwe. As it happened on the day of the memorial for Steve Biko I went to Groote Schuur Hospital to see the Prof. He had just had a major operation to remove a large section of his diseased lung. And there he was sitting in a comfortable chair, with that quite inimitable smile, speaking rather hoarsely and making little of his anguish. You know, we have often prostituted the English language so that we find we have to use quite outlandish superlatives to make our points, because ordinary straightforward words are now so hackneyed that they have lost their original significance. Hence Hollywood will tell us of a stupendous extravaganza and what have you. Despite this devaluation of language, I want to speak soberly without superlatives.

When you met Robert you knew without a shadow of doubt that you had met a great man. He had an outstanding intellect and yet walked with the humblest who felt at home in his company. He was too great to have a base or mean thought, and so quite amazingly he was untouched by bitterness, despite the unjust and cruel experiences he underwent for what he believed with all the fibre of his being. Even his most determined opponents had to admit that his was an attractive and magnetic personality. All who met him fell under the spell of his irresistible smile and charm. Even the Security Police ate out of his hand. They could not help it. He had the gentleness of a dove and yet he had the unshaken firmness of the person of principle. The years on Robben Island failed to change his beliefs.

I don't use these words lightly or glibly. He was a holy man, devoted to Jesus Christ his Lord and Master, and for that reason committed to seeing radical change happening in South Africa without violence and bloodshed, death and destruction. The tragedy of this country is that the powers that be have consistently refused to parley with such as Robert. And they may still live to regret missing such a grand opportunity, because they can't say of Robert what they said of Steve—that he was a virtual unknown —for Robert was a considerable political force to reckon with. And all South Africa could do with one of the greatest of her sons was to muzzle him, to banish and attempt to emasculate. What tragic and unmitigated waste. But when the annals of this our beloved country are rewritten, the name of Robert Mangaliso Sobukwe will be etched in letters of gold—for despite what they tried to do to him his spirit and his ideas broke through these fetters, and transcended the human restraints, and his spirit and his thoughts have lived on in the Black Consciousness Movement. I am sad that the University of the Witwatersrand, which was privileged because he taught there, never thought to honour one of the brightest stars in its firmament, and I hope that institution may still rectify this ghastly omission by a posthumous award.

And what about us? Must we mourn—Yes, to some extent for the going hence of a human being diminishes each of us. But let us not mourn disconsolately and long, because Robert would not have it so. We have offered in sacrifice some of the best of our people, and our struggle for justice, and for the ending of oppression and exploitation, is a moral struggle, and God is on our side. Robert knew he was part of a winning side. Victory is assured. Freedom is coming to South Africa for all of us. About that there is no doubt. God has assured us of this—our God, the liberator God of the Exodus. The questions still to be answered are how and when freedom will come. Robert worked and prayed that it would come soon and come peacefully. And we are with him in this struggle and prayer.

16. Polarisation

The Tate–Coetzee fight was the first occasion that a South African (white) fought for the World heavyweight boxing title.

I AM really distressed at the degree of polarisation that exists in our country. Last year I was working away until about midnight one Saturday night when the quiet of Soweto was shattered by car hooters blaring, and general pandemonium of the sort we associate with New Year's Eve in the townships. Then I remembered—it was the big Tate–Coetzee fight. 'I'm sure Tate has won', I said to myself. I switched on the radio (I hardly ever listen to the SABC. We vowed in our house that we would not get a TV set until the SABC provides us with a propaganda-free service). And my guess was confirmed. Most blacks in South Africa were thrilled that Tate had won (even those who were totally opposed to Tate's coming to fight in South Africa in the first place). They were thrilled because Tate was black, but also because he had made a South African white bite the dust. Most whites were despondent as a result of that defeat. It was as if it was a defeat on the battlefield. It certainly was more than just a sporting event for both sides. Somehow it was seen on one side as a blow against the so-called traditional South African way of life, and on the other as a slightly traumatic happening—something not too good for the South African white psyche.

I could go on to give a whole sorry catalogue of issues on which we are sadly divided on racial lines. On the matter of foreign investments most whites are in favour of increased investments, whereas I suspect (you can't speak about this openly) most blacks would wish to use this as a means for exerting pressure for real and meaningful change. Most whites were delighted when the British Lions came; not so blacks. Most whites were overjoyed that Margaret Thatcher's Conservative party came to power, and you can be sure that most blacks were saddened by this election result. Actually you could become a kind of Euclid and propound an axiom: whatever pleases most white South Africans is almost certain to displease most blacks and vice versa.

17. Banned people

Banning orders are frequently used to silence opponents of apartheid. Those who are banned may be subjected to house arrest, cannot associate or communicate with more than one person, and their articles, recordings or books cannot be quoted or distributed in South Africa. Just how petty and inhuman the banning orders are is well illustrated by the following story, told by Bishop Tutu in a sermon preached in Kingston, Jamaica, on the feast of Epiphany, 1979.

I VISITED one of these banned people, Winnie Mandela. Her husband, Nelson Mandela, is serving a life sentence on Robben Island, our maximum security prison. I wanted to take her Holy Communion. The police told me I couldn't enter her house. So we celebrated Holy Communion in my car in the street in Christian South Africa. On a second occasion I went to see her on a weekend. Her restriction order is more strict at weekends. She can't leave her yard. So we celebrated Holy Communion again in the street. This time Winnie was on one side of the fence and I on the other. This in Christian South Africa in 1978.

18. Detention without trial

Under the Terrorism Act of 1967, the police in South Africa have the power to detain opponents of apartheid indefinitely, without any access to families, solicitors or courts. And as if that was not enough, people often emerge from detention to find they have had a banning order served on them. This is a press statement, dated 20 November 1978.

WE REJOICE in the release of several people at the weekend from lengthy periods of detention. But why in God's name should they then be banned for five years without the opportunity of stating their side of the case?

The police have had more than enough time—394 days—to build cases against these people. Our deepest distress is that so very few white South Africans seem to care about this abrogation of the rule of law. We appeal yet again to the authorities of this land to move our society away from the brink of disaster. If whites do not care, God cares.

19. Urban unrest

Press statement, 17 June 1980.

WE DEPLORE all the violence that erupted over the weekend and we regret especially the death of one policeman. But we want to emphasise firmly that to tell people when they can mourn, and when they can't, is really to ask for trouble. The black community has been very deeply hurt by this insensitive ban on what have always been in the past peaceful, dignified, and solemn occasions. Afrikaners would be angered if one day they were told they cannot commemorate the day of the Covenant.

Please for God's sake let us stop playing with fire. I want to warn the authorities that their efforts at maintaining law and order will succeed only in producing a sullen and bitter lull. The situation in our country is highly volatile, and only meaningful discussions between the Prime Minister and at least Church leaders, with the intention of bringing about real change in South Africa, can deal with a rapidly deteriorating situation. We appeal with all our eloquence at our command for such a meeting. The black community can be dealt with effectively only through its own recognised leaders. Anything else the Government attempts will be like fiddling while the fires of revolution burn in our country.

We place ourselves unreservedly at the disposal of the authorities to work with them for justice, peace, law and order and reconciliation. Please will somebody hear us, please hear us before it is too late.

20. Armed soldiers on routine police matters

Press statement, 3 April 1978.

LAST FRIDAY 31 March, the police carried out a combined operation with the army and traffic police in what one newspaper described as a blitz. The police have to do their duty to maintain law and order, and to apprehend all lawbreakers and criminals. But I wish to express considerable disquiet that in carrying out their normal duties the police should have been assisted by army personnel armed with rifles and fixed bayonets. A senior police officer is reported to have described this combined operation as 'routine'. Nowhere in the free world is such a practice regarded as routine, when there is no civil disturbance or breakdown of law and order.

In the name of God and good sense, I want to appeal to the authorities to desist from the practice of employing armed soldiers on routine police matters. What happened on Friday can only be described as a very provocative action—many of those who were stopped were very tired, ordinary, decent law-abiding people, intent on getting home quickly out of the rain.

I want to protest very strongly about the body searches carried out on women by those manning the road blocks. One of my senior staff was subjected to this humiliating indignity. The police and authorities require the co-operation and assistance of the public in their difficult work of preventing crime, but last Friday's action was not calculated to win them any friends in the black community.

21. A better approach

Ever since the Soweto riots of June 1976, the anniversaries of 16 June have been occasions fraught with tension. The behaviour of the police on these occasions is often a contributory factor in the outbreak of violence, and following one such anniversary when the police were careful not to antagonise those who attended the memorial services, Bishop Tutu praised them for sensible conduct.

ON BEHALF of the South African Council of Churches, I wish to commend the police very warmly for keeping a very low profile during the services commemorating 16 June.

As many responsible blacks have pointed out in the past, there were hardly any incidents to mar what were mainly peaceful and dignified observances. We hope this is a style the police will adopt more and more to the benefit of our country.

22. The Pass Laws

The Pass Laws are designed to keep the black population 'in their place', by controlling their movement; restricting them to the 'homelands' or to the townships where they have the status of migrant labourers, or to short stays in adjoining 'white' urban areas. The Pass Laws are the mechanism by which white South Africa keeps the wealth and property of the country in its own hands, shutting blacks out from the industrial areas where employment and money are concentrated. The Pass Laws deliberately destroy family life, usually denying the migrant worker the right to have his family with him, and exemplify the convoluted thinking upon which apartheid is based. (The abolition of the Pass Laws in 1986 in theory removed government control over the movement of the black population. However, black South Africans require a work permit to travel into 'white' areas, and so still experience government control over their movements.) This is a Press statement from 1979.

NINETEEN YEARS ago, blacks protested peacefully for the abolition of the Pass Laws, which are the most resented feature of a hated system. The passes, more than anything else in South Africa, demonstrate that the black person is a second class citizen in the land of his birth.

For a while it seemed that these Pass Laws were being administered with decreasing hardness, since pass raids were not apparently being carried out as conspicuously as formerly. But the statistics for 1978 show an increase of 100,000 in those arrested for pass offences. Pass raids are becoming once again a feature of the South African scene. Perhaps this is an attempt by the authorities to remove unemployed blacks from the urban areas—to dump them in the bantustans, so that it will be a case of out of sight, out of mind. But arrests are also being made among people who are obviously working, or are students—most of them not being given the time to produce their passes, in violation of a Supreme Court ruling.

It appears from this that there is a deliberate stepping up of the harassment of blacks, otherwise why carry out raids even amongst people returning from work?

With all the eloquence I can command I appeal to the authorities to stop this harassment and humiliation of black people. Pass raids are highly provocative in a situation where tension is growing, due to high unemployment amongst black people. In the name of God and of Christian charity, let us beware that we are not deliberately leading up to another disastrous confrontation between the black community and the police; with consequent bloodshed, loss of life, destruction of property, and violence.

I am distressed by the apparent silence of our white fellow South Africans, over these latest developments. All of this is being done in your name. Do you acquiesce in something that has such potentially disastrous consequences? Don't say you are impotent. You can do something if you are opposed to what is happening. Beware of the legacy of hatred that the police action is building up amongst blacks. Assist for God's sake, act for your children's sake and for South Africa's sake.

23. Christmas

Press statement, 20 November 1978.

CHRISTMAS is a season of goodwill, of joy, but for many in our beloved land it is also a bleak time, a time of watching others enjoy good things without themselves having anything to enjoy. It is a time when deprivation is all the more starkly realised by those who have little, because of the excesses of those who have so much.

We believe it is right to herald the birthday of our Lord and liberator with joy and thanksgiving. We believe also that joy is increased when shared with others, that thanksgiving is the more real the more it is shared.

In this spirit of sharing we would appeal to those in business and industry to make available vacation jobs for those young people who will shortly go on holiday. In these days of rising unemployment it is becoming more and more difficult for parents to afford to give their children adequate educational opportunities. For some young people their only hope of being able to further their education is by making extra money to help their parents. The SACC is receiving daily requests for such temporary employment, and would be most willing to act as a clearing agency, to fit applicants to available jobs.

We appeal for this season of goodwill to be shared, in the name of him whose coming we celebrate.

24. Crossroads

The first shanties of Crossroads, the camp in the Cape Province near the townships of Nyanga and Guguletu, were set up in February 1975. The people were subjected to constant harassment, with the whole dreary scene of mass arrests, pass raids, and destruction of shacks being acted out by the police. In February 1977 eviction notices were served, and in August 1977 one of the camps in the settlement was demolished. In November 1978, Dr Koornhof, the government minister, bowed to pressure from the world community, and declared he was 'willing to regularise the position' of the Crossroads camp, and granted a stay of execution of the eviction order. Crossroads was saved, but unfortunately this did not mean that the government had decided on a change of policy towards the squatter camps in the country. In August 1981, police evicted people from the Nyanga settlement, in yet another particularly heartless operation, that yet again exposed the moral bankruptcy of the apartheid system. (Press statement, 16 May 1978.)

I VISITED Crossroads twice last Wednesday. In the afternon I went to see the Mobile Clinic and the school; the children sang and one of their songs told why Crossroads and places like it have happened—'Matanzima has no money'—the homelands are not financially viable. And then I met some of those extraordinary women who have decided they are going to be what they said they were going to be when they took their marriage vows—husbands' wives. One of them said to me, when I asked what she would do when they demolished Crossroads: 'Umfundisi, we will just take our belongings and go elsewhere to start another camp. If they want my husband here, working for them, then they will have to want me and my children.' That is the spirit of Crossroads—a dignified confidence that they are right in wanting to be families.

The second time I visited Crossroads was in the evening of that Wednesday—I preached at the regular Wednesday evening service, which was started to show the solidarity of those who live in the townships, with the squatters. There were over 500 people in the Hall. I am quite sure that it is immoral and unchristian to want to destroy family life, *especially* in a country that has a public holiday called—'Family Day'. So I add my voice to those who plead with the authorities to change their minds, even at this late stage. Do not destroy Crossroads. You are destroying a community and South Africa cannot afford that.

51

25. R.14,000,000 and all that

A piece in reply to a journalist, who asked Bishop Tutu what he would do with a sudden windfall. It is dated 17 November 1978.

OF COURSE, you must pinch me to ensure that I am not really dreaming. Imagine R.14,000,000 to spend as I wish! Others, as we have come to learn, have had considerable practice in how to lighten their heavy load of shekels. I can assure you that I am just a rank amateur in this game and I will perform like a raw recruit. Because of my lack of experience I have decided that I want to put forward my basic ideas and let an expert work out the details. After all, that is what we do when we want to build a house. We go to the architect and let him have our ideas, then he translates our vision into reality.

The really crying need among our people is adequate housing. A house makes you feel you have arrived, that you belong, and that you are not a bird of passage. It gives you roots, so I would want to do my bit to ease the ghastly shortage of proper housing. And I don't mean just a matchbox structure. Our black people have shown, that given the opportunity and the right kind of assistance —which has almost always been available to whites, Indians and Coloureds, that they erect splendid buildings. I would want my kind of house to be one that filled its owners with a proper kind of pride.

Then I would want to invest in a scheme that would make community services available—of the kind that other sections of the South African population take for granted. I am talking about tarred streets, proper sewerage, paved sidewalks to save us from the dust that plays havoc with our health and our smartly polished shoes. I would want proper streetlighting, to make our townships less attractive to the denizens of night, who are encouraged to perform their nefarious tasks by our ill-lit streets. It goes without saying that my scheme would ensure that we had electrified townships, so that we did not have to spend so much on coal, candles and paraffin. The smog that hangs over our townships in the early morning and evenings would be a thing of the past.

Imagine the improvement in our health, that we would register almost immediately.

It would be a luxury, perhaps, but I think we appreciate beautiful things too. So I would invest some of my munificence in creating parks with flowers and trees and grass, for lovers to walk around in, arm in arm, and have laughing children gambolling like frisky lambs on the shaven lawns. You could even throw in a few swimming pools, tennis courts and playgrounds to keep our children off the streets. I would want to see more libraries and places where people could learn wholesome hobbies.

I would then put most of what remained after my community 'binge' into education—into pre-school crèches, into well-built and well-equipped primary schools with libraries and, wonder of wonders, well-equipped laboratories. *We learned Science by imagining the various experiments.* I would keep some of the education funds for bursaries, to enable our children to further their education, here and abroad.

I would keep some of my funds to help get people out of the claustrophobic atmosphere of South Africa—get them to meet other people in different parts of the world so that they could experience what it means to be really human. It is a liberating experience.

I would leave a little to pay the accountant to see that I did not fiddle the books.

26. Black consciousness and car driving

An article of 9 November 1978, arising from the daily journey from the township of Soweto to work in Johannesburg.

LONG LINES of traffic, interminably snaking along from the different parts of Soweto early in the morning. Everybody is on their way to join the rat-race in their different places of work.

Tempers get frayed, exhausts belch thick black smoke, scooters are the only things that seem to make any headway.

We repeat this saga of the process of cars, buses, lorries and combies in the evening as we rush home—home with the haze hanging over our houses. I wish Soweto could be electrified. Our health for one thing would benefit, and just think of the saving, the cleanliness and the general improvement in our lives.

Here we are all sitting in this slow moving line of cars, trying to look unflustered, and gaining credit for developing the virtue of patience, when quite suddenly you see these cars—almost all of them taxis—flashing past this long line. They are travelling where the oncoming traffic is supposed to move. Sometimes you can see the traffic that is moving in the opposite direction flashing its headlights, to show these maverick cars the recklessness of their driving. Sometimes the cars which have the right of way are forced to swerve out of the way of these smart drivers. They obviously think that those who snake along slowly are stupid, and yet their driving is reckless, and they are endangering the lives of other road users. No wonder we have such ghastly accidents in and around our townships.

What is the remedy? A short term remedy would be to have traffic policemen patrolling these routes during the rush hours, ticketing the reckless drivers without mercy. But that is an unsatisfactory solution. Much the best solution is that we blacks show that we do have a proper pride in ourselves—that is what black consciousness is all about. We have a proper pride and self respect. And if I respect myself, then I will respect other blacks. And that respect has a great deal to do with how I drive. Why don't these smart drivers do their awful thing in town? Well, they are afraid of whites and they really despise themselves and other blacks. They need to be spiritually liberated not to despise themselves or other blacks.

That is black consciousness and car driving.

54

27. A message to journalists

The following two passages, dealing with the role of the press in society, both contain references to the 'Muldergate' affair. This political scandal involved Dr Connie Mulder, ex-Minister of Information, who was exposed as running a slush fund from which clandestine payments were made to promote South Africa's image at home and abroad. Allegations started appearing in the South African press in 1977 about the existence of this fund, which, it was suggested, had funded the pro-government Citizen *newspaper, as well as paying out large sums to politicians in Britain and the USA to protect South African interests. By the end of 1978 further leaks to the press conclusively proved Dr Mulder's involvement, and in April 1979 he was forced to resign his ministerial post and later his membership of Parliament. The scandal continued with the revelation that State President Vorster had also been centrally involved, and he was forced to resign as well. The amount of money involved was R.64 million (about £30 million).*

I THINK to be a journalist is a vocation, a calling filled with the joys of work well done, and the frustration of being often impeded in your search after the truth. There are those who do not want the truth to have too much scope, because truth can often be a dangerous commodity. It can make or break men and women, as we very well know from recent history in the United States and our own country, in those episodes known as Watergate and Muldergate. Yours *is* a high calling, because you are searchers after truth, and when you have found it, you are obliged to disseminate it, as far as is humanly possible, without distortion or embellishment. It can be a very costly and demanding vocation, because the powerful are not loath to use their power to crush those who have information which could have embarrassing or even disastrous consequences for them. I want to commend you as a fraternity for trying to be true to the highest ideals and traditions of your profession, as when you refuse to be intimidated into conformity, or into breaking confidences, even if to do so might land you in jail.

You are watchdogs for the nation, especially for the little men and women who can be manipulated, and treated shabbily by those who have power. You have an almost religious duty to come out on their behalf, to be like the Church of Jesus Christ; the voice of the voiceless, speaking up against the abuse of power, and standing up for the victims of oppression, exploitation and injustice. You must be the eyes of a society so often lulled into complacency, so that it can look and *see* how God's children are shunted from pillar to post, or left to starve, just because a racist ideology decrees that their community must be destroyed, because it is a black settlement on white land. You must be the ears of a society whose hearing has grown dull, so that it can hear the anguished cries of black mothers and children, left behind in an unviable, barren 'homeland', trying to eke out a miserable existence in some rural backwater, because South Africa's economy is based on the Migratory Labour System—a system that even the white Dutch Reformed Church condemned as a cancer in our society.

You have a crucial role to play in a South Africa that is in crisis. Whether you like it or not, you are powerful people and you help form public opinion. Many people read nothing beyond their newspapers. Many people, especially in South Africa, have seldom exercised their critical faculties, and so hardly ever question what they read. You carry a heavy responsibility. Some of the things you write may not seem too important, yet they go a long way to forming attitudes and perceptions.

I recall how many years ago the English press described an accident like this: 'Three persons and one native were injured'—giving unconscious expression to and confirming whites in their belief that 'natives' were human but . . . I am sure the fact that most newspapers nowadays address everybody, black and white, as Mr or Miss or Mrs must have an effect on racial attitudes, even if that effect is imperceptible.

Nobody can doubt that you help to reinforce certain points of view when you describe particular groups either as terrorists or freedom fighters or insurgents. I can only pray that God will give you courage and wisdom, because what you write, and how you write it, will have an important bearing on the future of our beloved country.

28. The black journalist and the black community

How is it possible to say that David Livingstone discovered the Victoria Falls? Weren't there people who had seen the Falls, perhaps every day of their lives, before Livingstone's so-called discovery? It was a discovery for *whites*, and history was written to fit in with their world view.

I am saying that you have an obligation to give the truth, and nothing but the truth, but from a black perspective. I also believe that you have an obligation to work for the liberation of our people. You must be involved in the Black Consciousness Movement, which seeks to remind blacks of their tremendous heritage as the children of God, that they are not faint carbon copies of others, but are each a glorious original, that they are of immense and indeed infinite value in the sight of God.

I remember vividly how I was inspired as a youngster by reading the black American journal *Ebony*. It warmed the cockles of my heart, as I contemplated the odds against achieving anything worthwhile, reading about those brothers and sisters in the US, who had made it, also against daunting odds. I didn't know anything about baseball then, but I thrilled at Jackie Robinson's achievement of breaking into the major league, by playing for what were then called the Brooklyn Dodgers. How many of us grew inches because of films such as *Stormy Weather*? I don't think it was particularly memorable, but it had an all black cast, and wasn't that something in those far off days?

You have a tremendous role to play in lauding black achievement, and telling our people that we *can* make it against all kinds of odds, and that the sky is the limit. We must be proud of you—so they can't say, 'We told you so—these blacks are irresponsible'. In your failure we all fail. If you succeed—'Oh he is exceptional'. Never mind. Don't fail us. You wield something they reckon is stronger than the sword—the pen. South Africa spent R.64,000,000 beause she thought so to some extent.

29. An Easter message

NOTHING COULD have been deader than Jesus on the Cross on that first Good Friday. And the hopes of his disciples had appeared to die with his crucifixion. Nothing could have been deeper than the despair of his followers when they saw their Master hanging on the Cross like a common criminal. The darkness that covered the earth for three hours during that Friday symbolised the blackness of their despair.

And then Easter happened. Jesus rose from the dead. The incredible, the unexpected happened. Life triumphed over death, light over darkness, love over hatred, good over evil. That is what Easter means—hope prevails over despair. Jesus reigns as Lord of Lords and King of Kings. Oppression and injustice and suffering can't be the end of the human story. Freedom and justice, peace and reconciliation, are his will for all of us, black and white, in this land and throughout the world. Easter says to us that despite everything to the contrary, his will for us will prevail, love will prevail over hate, justice over injustice and oppression, peace over exploitation and bitterness.

The Lord is risen. Alleluia.

PART FOUR

Freedom is Coming

In Part Four Tutu looks at the reasons why apartheid cannot continue indefinitely, and in the final piece, describes the vision of a free South Africa that helps to sustain his opposition to apartheid.

30. The certainty of freedom

The text of an article, dated 8 November 1978.

WE OFTEN hear it said that people learn from history—not to repeat the mistakes of the past and to benefit from the experience of others. But a cynic, looking at our sorry record, declared: 'We learn from history that we don't learn from history'. There is much evidence to support that remark. We have a wonderful capacity for self-deception. When we are driving along our roads we see the wrecks that lie about our roadsides—cars that for one reason or another have come to grief. Almost always we tell ourselves that that could not happen to me—it always happens to others, doesn't it?

I write in this vein to set the backdrop to my belief—that the liberation and freedom of the blacks in this land are inevitable. And the liberation of blacks involves the liberation of the whites in our beloved country, because until blacks are free, the whites can never be really free. There is no such thing as separate freedom—freedom is indivisible. At the present time we see our white fellow South Africans investing much of their resources to protect their so-called separate freedoms and privileges. They have little time left to enjoy them as they check the burglar proofing, the alarm system, the gun under the pillow and the viciousness of the watchdog. These resources could be employed in more creative ways to improve the quality of life of the entire community. Our white fellow South Africans think that their security lies in possessing a formidable and sophisticated arsenal of weapons. But they must know in their hearts that the security of all of us consists in a population whose members, black and white, are reasonably contented because they share more equitably in the good things of life, which all, black and white, have co-operated to produce.

So why do I believe that black liberation is inevitable? Or to put it another way: 'Why do I believe that real change, not just cosmetic change, is inevitable?' I believe this to be so because even the government thinks it must happen. Long ago, oh so long ago, we were told that South Africa was moving away from discrimination based on race. Nearly everybody is agreed that change is necessary. The former Prime Minister, Mr Vorster, saw this so clearly that he declared that if it did not happen, we would all be faced with the alternative too ghastly to contemplate.

But more fundamentally, I believe history teaches us a categorical lesson: that once a people are determined to become free, then nothing in the world can stop them reaching their goal. In the eighteenth century, Great Britain enjoyed a hegemony that extended to what came to be called the New World. She ruled over the thirteen Colonies of North America, as their Mother Country. These Colonies began to chafe at the bit, to find their colonial status galling. They had heard a British Parliamentarian pleading the case for their independence, and proclaiming: 'Taxation without representation is tyranny'. When their appeals for self-determination appeared to fall on deaf ears, then the thirteen Colonies, these puny things, threw the gauntlet down to the intimidating British Empire. The struggle seemed wholly unequal, but in the end, the thirteen Colonies emerged victorious against formidable odds. Nobody would have thought that when they signed their Declaration of Independence on 4 July 1776, that the thirteen Colonies would emerge the victors, thereby laying the foundation for the present day United States of America.

There are many other examples from history. France, through the French Revolution with its slogan of Liberty, Fraternity and Equality, when the exploited, against all the odds, overturned an oppressive system. In modern times we have had the Civil Rights movement in the USA, and the emergence out of colonial bondage of the so-called Dark Continent. Then there was the extraordinary resistance of the peasant people of Vietnam, who frustrated the efforts first of France, and then, incredibly, of the most powerful nation in the world—the USA—who were made to bite the dust in this struggle for the right to self-determination of a small people. My last reference is from the history of the Afrikaners. They believed themselves to be victims of British exploitation and misunderstanding. And we know what eventually happened. They triumphed so that today they are at the pinnacle of their power.

It seems, therefore, to be a universal law that when a people decide to become free, then absolutely nothing will eventually prevent them from reaching their goal. Why should it be thought that we blacks in South Africa will prove the exceptions to this rule?

For those among our people who feel despondent and hopeless, I want to assert that we shall be free. Do not despair of this. We shall be free because our cause is a just cause. We do not want to dominate others. We just want to have our humanity acknowledged. Our freedom is not in the gift of the white people. They cannot decide to give or to withhold it. Our freedom is an inalienable right bestowed on us by God. And the God whom we worship has always shown himself to be one who takes sides. He is a God who opposes evil and injustice and oppression. He is a God who sides with those who are oppressed because he is that kind of God, and not because the oppressed are morally better than their oppressors. And in setting at liberty the oppressed and exploited, he will also set free those who are enslaved by their human sinfulness. Let us rejoice. Let us lift up our heads and straighten our drooping shoulders. God cares and God will act decisively to bring justice, peace and reconciliation in our land. We will walk, black and white together, into this new South Africa, where people will matter because they are persons of infinite value, created in the image of God, the liberator God.

31. The black mood today

The Silverton raid was an ANC operation—an attack on a bank—that developed into a siege during which three ANC men were killed.

A FEW weeks ago one of the gunmen involved in the Silverton Raid was buried in Soweto. 15,000 people attended the funeral—most of whom were young blacks. Their perceptions were quite different from those of most whites, who regarded the dead man as a terrorist—the blacks honoured him and his companions as heroes. I am sure those who attended the funeral knew they would have to run the gauntlet of squads of policemen; that they might have their eyes smarting from tear-gas, and that they might well have to escape the snapping jaws of vicious police dogs. And yet they came in their thousands, with clenched fists beating against the skies, and their throats pouring forth what we call our freedom songs. 'Let them leave alone our land.' 'God give us strength, give us strength not to fear, give us strength because we need it.'

I want to point out something most whites and quite a few black adults do not yet know. And it is this. We really have a new breed of black exemplified by the young people who turned up at the funeral of the Silverton gunman. We of an older generation are on the whole still scared of arrest, of police dogs, of tear-gas, of prison and of death. But these young people are quite something else. They have experienced it all—yes, they have seen friends, brothers and sisters die and they are no longer scared. They are just determined. They are determined that they are going to be free, they and their reluctant cowed parents. They have, they believe, sat for too long, listening night after night to the stories of their parents' daily humiliations just because they were black. They have decided that enough is enough, and so they are people with iron in their souls. They are determined with a new kind of determination. Most of them believe that the goal which they are determined to reach—true liberation in what they call a united Azania—can come only with bloodshed and violence. They say this, and that is what is so shocking, in a matter of fact kind of way, for they say their leaders have tried everything peaceful and they have nothing to show for their efforts.

The determination of these young people has rubbed off on their parents, who are becoming politicised by so many things—the growing frustration with unemployment, the long queues to get 'influxed', the humiliation of pass raids, the inequities of the educational system, the travel on overcrowded buses and trains—one could go on much longer with this litany of woe. They too are getting more angry as they see so much wealth existing cheek by jowl with their poverty, and Mr Mugabe's victory in Zimbabwe has had an electrifying effect on blacks—most of whom whooped with real joy when they saw the goal of freedom being achieved. They are wondering how long they can go on believing change will come peacefully, when all the evidence seems to point in the other direction. The country is becoming more effectively armed, the authorities take action against all real leaders who want peaceful change, the pass laws are being more strictly applied, and many people are still being moved out to starve in the 'homelands'. There is bitterness and anger and hatred, which could easily develop into an all engulfing explosion.

Two years ago I spoke at Pietermaritzburg about reasonably peaceful change. After the meeting a black youngster, about twelve years old, said 'Father, I heard what you said, do you believe it?' I said 'Yes, though sometimes I hold on to this belief by the skin of my teeth'. He replied: 'Show me what you have achieved with all your talk of peaceful change, and I will show you what we gained with just a little violence'.

I will give one more example of the determination amongst our young black people. Some time ago I appeared in mitigation in a court in Pretoria. The accused—twelve people were on trial for allegedly taking part in military training—had asked that Revd Buti or I should come to plead in mitigation for them. Revd Buti was unable to go, so I was greatly privileged to appear instead. I say greatly privileged advisedly, as you will hear.

Some of the accused were young, and they had spent nearly sixteen months in custody. We don't know what was done to them during that time, but part of that time was spent in the maximum security section of Pretoria prison. This is the section that contains the death cells, which are hardly empty as far as blacks are concerned. So I thought I would see people who had had the stuffing knocked out of them. And on that morning six of them who had been found guilty knew that the hangman's noose was hanging over their heads. But what did we find? Just before the judge came in it was these accused who were the most vivacious people in the court.

One of the accused said this in his statement, before sentence was passed. 'Your Lordship, I went into this with my eyes open. I

65

have a vision of a new South Africa, where people count because they are human, and where the colour of one's skin is irrelevant. The tragedy is that it will cost so much to bring this South Africa about. I am young and recently married; we have one child. I would like to be with my wife and have more children. But I am ready to accept whatever penalty you wish to impose on me. I may not enjoy this new South Africa, but my brother will.'

32. The impact of the Soweto riots

The riots in the township of Soweto, five miles from Johannesburg, caused widespread unease amongst the white population. On 16 June 1976, thousands of schoolchildren marched against a decree ordering an increase in the use of Afrikaans in schools. Rioting, which spread through South Africa, broke out when police shot and killed thirteen-year-old Hector Peterson. About 500 young black people were killed in the troubles, which lasted from June 1976 to January 1977.

MANY COMMENTATORS, when asked to give their assessment of the South African situation after 16 June 1976, replied with a well-worn cliché. 'South Africa will never be the same again.' It is a hackneyed expression, but it has been proved to be only too true by subsequent events.

Before that fateful day most of us declared that anybody trained in the Bantu education system, could be little other than a docile, unthinking conformist. We did not think they were capable of protesting in such a disciplined manner. And yet it was precisely those children, who had been fed on the thin gruel that passed for education, who said in no uncertain terms: 'We have had enough. We are God's children made in his image, and we demand our birthright of an educational system equal to that for children of other racial groups in South Africa.'

Yes, those children took everyone by surprise, including their own parents. Even the Security Police, who have riddled our community with a network of informers, were caught with their pants down—quite unprepared for what the children had decided to do. We now know that the issues of education, and the attempted imposition of the Afrikaans language, were merely the immediate causes of the students' anger. Their protest meant that they rejected the entire apartheid system of legalised inferiority, oppression, injustice and exploitation. They were saying: 'We belong to South Africa, and we are going to have our rightful share of all her resources—social, political, economic and educational. We are not going to apologise for our existence. God did not make a mistake in creating us black, and we are going to participate in all the forms of decision making—especially political—which affect our lives. Nothing is going to stop us becoming free; our freedom is a gift from God and not something that whites can withhold or grant as they wish.'

That message has gone the length and breadth of our beautiful and beloved land. Four years later it was taken up by so-called Coloureds protesting against a third class citizenship. Now there is this new determination abroad. All blacks (Indians, Coloureds, Africans) know they are all oppressed. You can't have a woman who is half pregnant. You are either oppressed or privileged. So we have a new solidarity to add to the determination that we shall all be free, black and white together, and nothing but just nothing can stop us. There are many who would suffer imprisonment, exile or even death to attain the glorious goal of true freedom for all in a united South Africa. We are called to work for true freedom and liberation for all—otherwise we will perish in the alternative too ghastly to contemplate.

Nkosi sikelel' iAfrika—Morena Boloka sechaba sa heso (God bless Africa). Let it be so (Makubenjalo). Yes, South Africa can never be the same again, because of what happened on 16 June 1976.

33. Free Nelson Mandela

Nelson Mandela's epic imprisonment (1962–90) brought him world-wide fame, and confirmed his position as spokesman for South Africa's black majority. Born in 1918, he worked as a lawyer in Johannesburg, and led the Defiance Campaign against Unjust Laws of 1952. He was put on trial in 1956 for treason, with 155 others, but everyone was eventually acquitted in 1960. After Sharpeville he went under-ground, and became known as the 'Black Pimpernel', continuing to organise in South Africa. He went abroad in 1962, to try and gain support from African heads of state and politicians in London. But soon after he returned to South Africa he was arrested and sentenced to five years for inciting strikes, and leaving the country without a valid passport. Following a police raid on the secret ANC headquarters in Rivonia—a district of Johannesburg—he was taken from his cell to face trial with eight others on charges of sabotage, and conspiracy to overthrow the government. One man was acquitted, but the eight men found guilty, including Mandela, were sentenced to life imprisonment.

This is the text of an address delivered at Natal University on 28 April 1980.

MY OPINION is that we are going to have a black Prime Minister in South Africa within the next five-to-ten years. No serious minded person today thinks that it is possible for a group outnumbered five to one, as the white community is by blacks, can go on forever lording it over the majority. All the logic of history is against such a thing happening.

Also, recent years have seen significant developments in the white community in South Africa. We used to think that the Afrikaner community, which has produced our rulers, was a monolithic, immovable structure, which would resist any efforts to reduce its power as a united group. That is not the case any longer. There are unprecedented rumblings within the Afrikaans Church; the very Church which has always provided the religious and moral justification for the existence of the Afrikaner community. There is no longer that awesome solidarity and unanimity within the religious manifestation of the Afrikaner community.

The Information Scandal ('Muldergate') shook many of the more principled members of the Afrikaans community. For some it was not merely disillusioning, it was positively traumatic; shaking the foundations of their belief that though their policies might sometimes cause hurt, they were basically morally justifiable. It could be that once they realise that apartheid can no longer be justified scripturally, that they throw caution to the winds, saying any method that ensures their survival is justified. It could also be that if they were threatened by a common foe, they would all rush into the laager. But what I am trying to stress is that we no longer have a united mass, which knows where it is going or how to get there. That will have significant political consequences.

Do I need to point out that the Afrikaner psyche has also been shaken by Afrikaans writers and literary men, who, with apparent intransigence, have declared that they find censorship intolerable? What about the Afrikaans press, which has been heard to say that whites must be ready to share what they have, or risk losing it all? Or even saying that the authorities should speak to the *real* leaders of the black community. This is a different kind of Afrikaans community, slightly more awake as disaster stares them in the face. We should not get too enthusiastic, but these are the pointers to the changes occurring in Afrikanerdom.

The Prime Minister has been saying things that we would not have expected from a Nationalist Prime Minister. He has been saying 'Adapt or die', and he is a realist, who has been told by his military advisors that there is no way the white community can win a war, conventional or unconventional, with 80% of the population disaffected. I have concentrated on the Afrikaners for the simple reason that they hold the key to political power, and that in the end the discussion is going to have to be between the Afrikaners and the blacks.

Blacks may not have much military power. But we have our consumer power, and South Africa still depends to a large extent on our labour. We are not yet properly organised, but the latent power is there. Banning, detentions, banishments will not stop freedom coming. They merely postpone the inevitable, and build up a legacy of bitterness and hatred, which we could well do without, as we learned from Zimbabwe. Okay—there is going to be a black Prime Minister in South Africa within five-to-ten years. The white community cannot stop that happening. What the white community still has in its power to do is to decide whether that Prime Minister is going to end up there through a process of reasoned negotiation, and discussion at a conference table, or whether he will have to do so after bitter fighting and bloodshed. I think we have a very good chance of pulling off the first alternative. And we need Nelson Mandela, because he is almost certainly going to be that first black Prime Minister. He represents all our genuine leaders, in prison and in exile. So to call for his release is really to say, please let us sit down, black and white together, each with our acknowledged leaders, and work out our common future, so that we can move into this new South Africa, which will be filled with justice, peace, love, righteousness, compassion and caring.

One would like to say to some politicians: 'learn at least one lesson from Zimbabwe—don't make such categorical statements. You will have to eat your words—look at Mr Ian Smith and his "no black majority rule in a 1,000 years".' It is possible that some politicians will end up being totally irrelevant. Retirement might do some of them good.

God loves us in South Africa very dearly. He has said, I want to give you an object lesson on how *not* to solve a political crisis—and he has unfolded before us the lesson of Zimbabwe. They could have been at this point in their history without the price of over 20,000 deaths, devastation, bitterness and hatred which they have had to pay. I think we can have a new non-racial South Africa, and that we can achieve it reasonably peacefully, but that means we must negotiate and bargain at the conference table, and this can only be done by genuine and acknowledged leaders. Hence our call, Free Mandela, and start talking.

34. Black consumer power—one lever for change

In addition to the power that blacks have as consumers, is the power of their labour, upon which South African prosperity is built. In recent years there has been a growth of trade unions amongst the black workforce, that has gained substantial support. The strike of the municipal workers of Johannesburg in 1980, when the entire workforce came out for more pay, was a sign that the new unions were making themselves felt, and could play an important role in bringing about a more just society.

This has been taken from an address given at the opening of the Black Chain Supermarket, Johannesburg, 16 February 1980.

TODAY WE have come to say 'thank you God', thank you for a black achievement. I want to underline black. I do so because there are many in our country, both black and white, who still believe that black people are not quite able to do these things. You often hear them say, if a black has succeeded, 'Ah well, he is exceptional'. And if a black fails, then they will say, almost with glee: 'What did you expect—I told you so'. But we have come here to thank God for this black achievement.

Our people should know their consumer power. Many businesses in Johannesburg would collapse if we withdrew our support. Many white newspapers, such as the *Rand Daily Mail* or the *Sunday Times*, would have their circulation drastically reduced if blacks stopped buying them. Many building societies and banks would feel a cold draught if we withdrew our savings. And yet they still often treat us as if *they* were doing us favours. For a long time blacks have not been able to get housing loans from building societies—yet our money has helped to subsidise white housing. The building societies and banks could have agitated for a change in the law long ago, like the wine farmers, who insisted that blacks should be allowed to drink the so-called white man's liquor.

We have to realise our consumer power, and let white South Africa know about it, so that they negotiate with us as those who have that power. Some of these newspapers I have mentioned report news that affects us—as if we did not form an important part of their readership! They write as if their readers were only white. We should ask them to consider for instance their use of the term 'terrorist', when there are neutral terms they could use. We should remind them that they get advertising because of their circulation figures, and that black readership boosts these figures. We want fundamental change in South Africa reasonably peacefully—let these newspapers and businesses urge their government to negotiate with blacks before it is too late, because blacks have power.

You businessmen must succeed in this venture for the sake of black liberation, which involves white liberation as well. As long as blacks are not free, no one will be free in South Africa. Freedom is indivisible. You business people must realise that you won't prosper if you think only of yourselves. Our poor and unemployed and unprosperous blacks will drag you back. We must move forward together. Our prosperity must be one we share with the black community—after all, if you help to increase our buying power you end up with busy tills. You must be concerned with the betterment of our people—giving scholarships for education, helping cultural and other projects, being involved in community development projects—for the sake of all of us in South Africa. I believe in an undivided South Africa where we all matter because God has created us in his image. He has planned us even before we were conceived. We are each a VSP—a very special person.

35. My vision for South Africa

From an article dated 25 March 1979.

WE SHOULD all have the freedom to become fully human. That is basic to my understanding of society—that God created us without any coercion, freely for freedom. Responsibility is a nonsense except in the context of freedom—freedom to accept or reject alternative options, freedom to obey or disobey. God, who alone has the perfect right to be a totalitarian, has such a tremendous respect for our freedom to be human, that he would much rather see us go freely to hell than compel us to go to heaven.

According to the Bible, a human being can be a human being only because he belongs to a community. A person is a person through other persons, as we say in our African idiom. And so separation of persons because of biological accidents is reprehensible and blasphemous. A person is entitled to a stable community life, and the first of these communities is the family. A stable family life would be of paramount importance in my South Africa.

There would be freedom of association, of thought and of expression. This would involve freedom of movement as well. One would be free to go wherever one wanted, to associate with whomsoever one wished. As adult humans we would not be subject to draconian censorship laws. We can surely decide for ourselves what we want to read, what films to view and what views to have. We must not be frogmarched into puritanism.

Because we are created in the image of God one of our attributes is creativity. South Africa is starved of the great things many of her children can create and do, because of artificial barriers, and the refusal to let people develop to their fullest potential. When one has been overseas and seen for example the Black Alvin Ailey dance group, which performed modern ballet to standing room only crowds at Covent Garden, then one weeps for how South Africa has allowed herself to be cheated of such performances by her own inhabitants. How many potentially outstanding people are being denied the opportunity to get on?

When I think of the splendid young people I have met, who despite some horrendous experiences at the hands of the system, have emerged quite unscathed with bitterness, and who have a tremendous humanity and compassion, then I weep because we are so wantonly wasteful of human resources. We need a course on human ecology.

I lay great stress on humaneness and being truly human. In our African understanding, part of Ubantu—being human—is the rare gift of sharing. This concept of sharing is exemplified at African feasts even to this day, when people eat together from a common

73

dish, rather than from individual dishes. That means a meal is indeed to have communion with one's fellows. Blacks are beginning to lose this wonderful attribute, because we are being inveigled by the excessive individualism of the West. I loathe Capitalism because it gives far too great play to our inherent selfishness. We are told to be highly competitive, and our children start learning the attitudes of the rat-race quite early. They mustn't just do well at school—they must sweep the floor with their rivals. That's how you get on. We give prizes to such persons, not so far as I know to those who know how best to get on with others, or those who can coax the best out of others. We must delight in our ulcers, the symbols of our success.

So I would look for a socio-economic system that placed the emphasis on sharing and giving, rather than on self-aggrandisement and getting. Capitalism is exploitative and I can't stand that. We need to engage the resources that each person has. My vision includes a society that is more compassionate and caring, in which 'superfluous appendages' [*the government's way of describing families of black workers*] are unthinkable, where young and old are made to feel wanted, and that they belong and are not resented. It is a distorted community that trundles its aged off into soulless institutions. We need their accumulated wisdom and experience. They are splendid for helping the younger to feel cared for; certainly that has been the experience in the extended family.

I believe too that in a future South Africa we must be supportive of the family. The nuclear family is not geared to stand all the strains placed on it by modern day pressures. There are things we can survive better in a group than singly. I know there are pressures in the extended family, but I need to be persuaded that these are greater than those presently haunting the nuclear family.

Basically I long and work for a South Africa that is more open and more just; where people count and where they will have equal access to the good things of life, with equal opportunity to live, work, and learn. I long for a South Africa where there will be equal and untrammelled access to the courts of the land, where detention without trial will be a thing of the hoary past, where bannings and other such arbitrary acts will no longer be even so much as mentioned, and where the rule of law will hold sway in the fullest sense. In addition, all adults will participate fully in political decision making, and in other decisions which affect their lives. Consequently they will have the vote and be eligible for election to all public offices. This South Africa will have integrity of territory with a common citizenship, and all the rights and privileges that go with such a citizenship, belonging to all its inhabitants.

Clearly, for many people, what I have described is almost a Utopia, and we cannot reach that desired goal overnight. Black leaders would, I feel, be willing to go back to the black community, and say: 'Hold on—things are moving in the right direction' if certain minimum conditions were pledged and met, even in stages, by the white powers that be. These are:

(A) Abolition of the Pass Laws.
(B) The immediate halting of population removals.
(C) The scrapping of Bantu Education, and a move towards a unitary educational system.
(D) A commitment to call a National Convention.

These would be significant steps towards realising the vision.

1. Nelson Mandela. His speech from the dock in the Rivonia trial is
   one of the classic statements of African nationalism. He was
   imprisoned from 1962 until his release in 1990.
   (*Photo: Eli Weinberg*)

2. Robert Sobukwe. 'When the
   annals of this our beloved country
   are rewritten, the name of
   Robert Mangaliso Sobukwe
   will be etched in letters of gold.'

3. Steve Biko. 'He had a far too
   profound respect for persons as
   persons, to want to deal with
   them under readymade,
   shopsoiled categories.'

4. Steve Biko's son Samora, his wife Ntsiki, and mourners at his funeral in King William's Town.

5. The procession at Steve Biko's funeral.

6. Part of Soweto. (*Photo: Abisag Tullman*)

7. A white residential area. (*Photo: Tony McGrath*)

8. Demonstrators lie dead after the police opened fire at Sharpeville.
(*Photo: Ian Berry*)

9. Troop carriers confront demonstrators in an incident during
the Soweto riots of 1976.

10. Children and the Crossroads squatter camp, 1978. (*Photo: Steve Bloom*)

11. Student groups who hijacked two buses on their way to the funeral of the 'Silverton Siege' three. (*Photo: RDM*)

12. Bishop Desmond Tutu, Mrs Leah Tutu, and the Revd Thomas Anthony, a visiting Canadian minister, leaving court after spending one night in police custody in John Vorster Square. (*Photos 1-12 courtesy of IDAF*)

13. Desmond Tutu receiving the Nobel Peace Prize in Oslo on 13 December 1984 from the Norwegian Nobel Committee chairman, Mr Egil Aavik. (*Photo: Press Association*)

14. Desmond Tutu speaking at a press conference in Johannesburg, 12 April 1986. (*Photo: Associated Press*)

PART FIVE

Looking to the Future

At the beginning of the 1980s Desmond Tutu outlined the challenges that he believed would face the Christian Church in future years. They ranged from the potential ecological crisis threatening humanity and the gap between rich and poor, to matters like Church unity and the ordination of women.

Looking to the Future

36. Survival as a human society

WE STAND at the beginning of a new decade that must surely be a crucial one for our survival as a human society. We have been warned often enough. When one reads books such as Toffler's *Future Shock* or the Club of Rome's *Limits to Growth*, one wishes that the future they predict would not come upon us. Their prognostications are so bleak and unattractive. We are warned that unless we take drastic action now, then we will have had it. They tell us that we face the danger of being overwhelmed by vast numbers, because of the approaching population explosion. There is, after all, only so much space available, and this space can accommodate only so many people at an optimum level of existence. Apart from the likely disappearance of space to house all the teeming millions that are likely to people the earth by the turn of the century, we are being warned that there is no way in which the earth will be able to produce enough food for all its inhabitants.

We have not been responsible stewards of our land resources; we have pillaged and plundered as if we could replenish the irreplaceable topsoil, that has been ravaged by wasteful agricultural methods. The earth's surface is being desecrated at an alarming rate.

As if that were not already serious enough, we are wantonly wasteful of our non-replenishable fossil fuel resources—our coal and oil and gas stockpiles are not inexhaustible. And whilst some may look hopefully at nuclear energy, we have been warned about the hazards of tampering with it—note the recent near disaster at the Harrisburg nuclear station in the USA. Moreover, nobody has yet come up with a solution to the problem of the disposal of nuclear waste, waste that has a long radio-active life.

Have you had enough? What about the threat of the mushroom cloud? We look on helplessly as country after country attains nuclear capability. We see the mad scramble of the arms race, the investment of scarce capital resources that could have been used in socially beneficial schemes.

There is an uneasy global equilibrium. The earth has perhaps never been more vulnerable than it appears to be in our day. The uneasy truce is always in grave danger of being broken, especially as we notice the gap between the affluent West (including Japan) and the poor so-called Third World. The gap is widening and augurs ill for the peace of the world. Our earth home is, it seems, always on the edge of a conflagration.

37. Future challenges: South Africa

The South African Prime Minister, Mr Botha, fought the 1981 white only election to gain a mandate for his policy of peripheral reforms to the apartheid system. These reforms, such as the international hotels mentioned (where black and white people can drink in the same bars) leave the structure of apartheid untouched, and go nowhere near to satisfying black aspirations in South Africa.

THERE CAN be no doubt at all that the most serious challenge facing the world today is not Communism, despite the adventures of Soviet Russia in Afghanistan, which have given South Africa a temporary breathing space. Most of the Westerners who have tended to have an obsession with the threat of world domination posed by Communism, would like us to believe that that is in fact the case. South Africa has capitalised on this by describing herself, and trying to project herself, as the last bastion of Christian Western Civilisation, against the predatory advances of Communism. It has passed such laws as the Suppression of Communism Act and other viciously repressive legislation, and many in the West have been duped. 'Communist' in South Africa has become the favourite swearword of those who support apartheid and the Nationalist government. Any opponent of apartheid could fall foul of the Suppression of Communism Act, even if he was known to be an ordained minister of a Christian denomination, who believed in God and who worshipped regularly. Very few in South Africa care to point out the blatant contradiction in all this.

We have had to tell our white fellow South Africans that for blacks, the immediate concern is not with Communism, however defined. For us it is but a future and hypothetical threat. Our priority concern as blacks, is the harsh reality of the present, which we experience every day of our lives at nearly every point. Our humanity is denigrated, called into question, and determined by an arbitrary criterion for which we cannot be praised or blamed —the colour of our skins. Our priority concern is that we are treated as less than third-grade citizens in the land of our birth, in an effort to keep political power in the hands of a small white oligarchy outnumbered five to one. It is a system of institutionalised violence, using migratory labour, which *deliberately*, not accidentally, destroys black family life. It is a system that uses structural unemployment, by having reservoirs of unskilled labour in the 'homelands', to provide cheap labour. It uses the institutionalised violence of forced population removals to keep black people in their place. Human beings are uprooted from areas where they have normally had adequate housing, and work of some sort, to be dumped as if they were sacks of potatoes in some God-forsaken arid area, many times without adequate alternative accommodation. They are usually too far from places of work, and so they sit there listlessly, 'waiting to die', as some of them have said.

They are sent to these resettlement camps to starve. It is not accidental. It is part of the government policy to remove the blacks from so-called white South Africa, so that these blacks can exercise their political rights in a soapbox opera land, with a spurious independence recognised only by white South Africa. This is done so that the whites can say that blacks have no claim to political representation in 'white' South Africa, because they are all aliens there.

I visited several of these resettlement camps. At one of them I saw a little girl, who lived with her widowed mother and sister, and asked:

'Does your mother get a pension or a grant?'
'No', she replied.
'Then what do you do for food?'

81

'We borrow food', she replied.

'Have you ever returned any of the food that you have borrowed?'

'No.'

'What do you do when you can't borrow food?'

'We drink water to fill our stomachs.'

That happens in a land that boasts that it can send maize to starving Zambia. This is the policy of apartheid, and that is how it intends to solve the political crisis in our land. *That* is the real challenge that stares the world in the face in the 1980s. What are you going to do about South Africa, which follows such an inhumane, such an evil and diabolical policy? I have already warned in South Africa that if the government are determined to go ahead with their population uprooting schemes, and their policy of depriving blacks of their South African citizenship, then we can kiss goodbye to any hopes of a reasonably peaceful solution, for which I and many others are working. We will be embroiled in a bloodbath, or what former Prime Minister of South Africa, Mr Vorster, called 'the alternative too ghastly to contemplate'.

There are only two options left for South Africa. One is for the white minority to hold on to all political power, making minor and peripheral adjustments—this leads as inexorably to violence and bloodshed as night follows day, and we must do everything to avert that national suicide. The other is that they agree that their salvation and true security lie in political power-sharing—this can still happen. Of course it will mean a declension in the very high standard of living that white South Africa enjoys. But we say they should be willing to give up something, rather than risk losing everything. Let them negotiate whilst they can do so from a position of strength, and whilst there are those amongst the blacks who still want to negotiate for a reasonably peaceful settlement. Every day that passes merely serves to erode further the credibility of those wanting to talk, and increase the acceptability of those who say the only language is the language of force.

The United Nations has declared that the apartheid system poses a threat to world peace. This would include the unresolved

82

situation in Namibia. What I am saying is that if a racial war were to erupt in South Africa, it could very well trigger off a Third World War. This is not being melodramatic, because we saw how the United States and the Soviet Union were in an eyeball to eyeball confrontation over Angola. South Africa is a much more coveted prize. In addition, as a senior US Senator told me in Washington DC, a racial upheaval in South Africa would have the most horrendous consequences for race relations in the USA. This would apply certainly also to Britain, where race relations are already on the boil. One might point out that several Western countries have significant concentrations of people from Third World countries. So the situation in those countries would not be left untouched by a South African racial explosion.

However, one knows that many Westerners, and this sadly includes their churches, are really loath to take decisive action against South Africa, action to ensure that there was a rapid evolution to majority rule. (Not *black* but *majority* rule.) In part it is because their kith and kin are involved, so they are affected in emotional ways. The West is also involved financially, so it feels that change could threaten their investments. They are embroiled with South Africa through military and especially nuclear collaboration (though they deny this vehemently). So one questions whether there is a real will to see fundamental change happening, without bloodshed and through the armed struggle. I am still hoping that we can persuade our Western brothers and sisters to exert all the diplomatic, political and economic pressure possible, to drive us to the conference table. But I sense a great deal of reluctance to exert this pressure, and too much enthusiasm to refer to changes that are supposedly happening under the Botha administration.

Mr P. W. Botha has a greater grasp of reality than most of his predecessors. But apartheid is not dead; we have not seen the corpse, or been invited to the funeral. People speak about changes in the sports arena, in so-called international hotels, in restaurants and cinemas which allow blacks admission together with whites, and of the removal of discriminatory signs. The best that can be said about all this is that they probably create a climate for change, and begin a process which it might be difficult to reverse. But most blacks see these as cosmetic, superficial changes, which do nothing for those who live in ghettos and travel in overcrowded trains and buses to and from work.

It is possible that the government may be beginning a new strategy, of doing away with discrimination based on race alone. It may be ready to co-opt some blacks, with substantial material privileges, who will then act as a buffer middle-class between the whites and the have-not blacks, and who will become vociferous supporters of the status quo that gives them so many privileges. It will then cease being just a race question. It will have become a class struggle. But social and economic concessions and privileges, however substantial, are always vulnerable since they depend on the whim of those who possess political power.

So surely the most immediate, most urgent, challenge for the 1980s is South Africa, until a more just and open non-racial society exists in that beautiful land.

38. The affluent West and the Third World

I WOULD place, as next on the agenda, the growing gap between the affluent, developed countries mainly found in the Northern hemisphere, and the abject poverty of the developing countries, found mainly in the Southern hemisphere. In the latter are to be found two-thirds of the world's inhabitants, who enjoy an infinitesimal percentage of the wealth of the globe we inhabit. There is a harshness in the rapacity of the industrialised giants, as they play havoc with ecology in their wanton exploitation of the resources of the earth. The wealthy consume a great deal more than can be justified by their population figures. But it will not be that the hungry masses will forever just look on at the groaning tables of their wealthy neighbours. This could be the next flashpoint. We from Africa will have to raise this question in international forums. We must call for a more equitable distribution and sharing of the good things of the earth, fair prices for our primary products, and more just competition in the markets of the world. I have no doubt that many who come from the poorer parts of the world have grown somewhat cynical about the so-called free enterprise system. In it some are certainly a great deal freer than others. From my perspective Capitalism seems to give unbridled licence to human cupidity, and has a morality that belongs properly to the jungle—'the survival of the fittest, the weakest to the wall, and the devil take the hindmost'. I find what I have seen of Capitalism and the free enterprise system quite morally repulsive. I long for a society which is not so grasping, not ruled by the laws of the rat-race, but one in which there is more sharing. I deplore the sort of society which is uncaring and selfish, and hope that we will work for a society that is more compassionate and caring, and values people not because they are consumers or producers, but because they are of infinite value, since they are created in the image of God.

So the second major challenge is posed by the gap between the rich developed world, and the vastly poorer developing world. If we are not careful it could be that starved men and women will march on empty stomachs, to invade the well-stocked larders of the wealthy. Desperate people use desperate methods. We will die as fools, if we cannot learn to live together as brothers—to paraphrase Martin Luther King.

39. A prophetic Church and human rights in the Third World

Archbishop Luwum was murdered in Uganda in February 1977, on the orders of Idi Amin, after he had presented a written petition on the question of human rights, which were being flagrantly violated with torture, murder and rape being practised by Amin's army.

THE CHURCH in Africa, and the Church in the Third World

generally, must come into its own. We know that the Church took a risky turn at the time of Constantine's conversion, when it became a licit organisation, allied with the State and the powerful. It did not always maintain a critical distance, so that it could carry out its prophetic ministry and say: 'Thus saith the Lord . . .'. The result was that the poor and the voiceless found themselves opposed by the very body that should have been on their side. It was all too easy for the Church to sanctify an unjust status quo, because it stood to benefit materially from its alliance with the high and mighty, totally unmindful of its vocation to be a serving Church.

In the newly independent Third World countries, we have often seen serious inroads into civil liberties and human rights. The position of the people has often been worse under their own rulers, than it ever was under their colonial masters. There is often no freedom of speech, or press freedom. Criticism of the abuse of power by largely totalitarian military dictatorships, is frowned on. Political dissent is not allowed, on the pretence that developing countries cannot afford the luxury of having a democratic system, or that one-party states are not necessarily dictatorships.

Unfortunately, there are very few such. One is worried that the lot of our Third World is such a hard one, with so few examples of peaceful transition from one set of political leaders to another. Corruption is rife, and the people, in their already impoverished condition, have to bear the brunt of all this. My worry is that the Church has by and large been too quiescent, seemingly afraid to rock the boat too much. There are splendid and glorious exceptions, such as Archbishop Luwum who confronted the evil Amin with the demands of the Gospel of Jesus Christ, and paid for this courageous act with his life—or the experience of Cardinal Malula in Zaire. My concern is for the integrity of the Church of Jesus Christ. We must be seen to be motivated, not by political considerations, but by the imperatives of the Gospel, speaking out that evil is evil, whether perpetrated by black or white. The Church must be willing to pay the price of its loyalty to its Lord and Master. Political leaders have often been let down by a sycophantic Church leadership, who should provide moral and ethical guidance, but who are content to be time-servers. The

Church in Africa is faced with this challenge of injustice, corruption, oppression and exploitation at home, and it has no option but to fulfil its prophetic vocation, or seriously call in question its claim to be the Church of Jesus Christ. We in Africa have much to learn here from the Church in Latin America, and also in South Korea.

Related to this question of the role of the Church *vis-à-vis* governments, is its stand over the growing gap between the rich, who grow ever richer, and the poor who grow ever poorer in our countries. The rich Africans become expert exploiters of fellow Africans, and the Church is tempted to side with the rich and the powerful, ignoring the poor, those whom Christ called the least of his brethren. We must move into the slums that are rising so quickly around our cities, we must minister to the prostitute and the down and out. We must be the Church of the poor and the marginalised ones, who have no power or voice. We must become their voice and strive to empower them, and help them help themselves so that they can enter into their heritage—the heritage of the freedom of the children of God, and a humanity that is measured by nothing less than the humanity of Jesus Christ himself.

40. Divided Churches

From a sermon preached at Bosmont, and an address on the subject of Church unity.

DURING THE 1970s I visited Northern Ireland; I had been invited to address the General Assembly of the Presbyterian Church in Ireland. Ulster, of course, has been wracked by a civil war between, on the one side, Protestant groups who want to remain linked to Britain, and who are the top dogs; on the other side there are the Roman Catholics who want to be united with Eire, where they would hope to enjoy a better deal than they do at present, as a somewhat deprived minority. We have been told times without number of the horrible casualties of this war—if you are a Protestant in a Roman Catholic area then your days are usually numbered and vice-versa. The brutality is often unbelievable.

While visiting that sadly divided land I was taken on a tour of Belfast. On the surface things looked quite normal. People were rushing to work, mothers were taking children to school, and doing their shopping. It all looked quite normal, until one looked at the buildings which had been gutted by fire, and the streets that had been scarred by bombs. It all looked quite normal until one saw the troop carriers, with soldiers holding guns, their fingers always on the trigger—then that air of the normal became quite eerie. I won't easily forget a particularly shattering sight which will remain etched on my memory—it was almost as if it had been set up for my benefit. At one street corner were two groups of children and youngsters, obviously belonging to the two opposing sides in the strife. They were taunting one another and throwing stones at one another.

At one level this quarrel was political—a matter of civil rights for a minority—but at another level it was religious, because the two sides belonged, one to the Roman Catholic Church, and the other to the various Protestant denominations. And look at what Christianity has done to the children. They belong to a faith that claims that its Lord and Master had broken down the middle wall of partition, and made all people one as members of his body, the Church. But looking at those children, all the protestations about reconciliation sounded so hollow.

During the Assembly one of the delegates described a horrifying incident. He told of some teenage girls who had gone to drink at a pub, then went on to stone to death a girl belonging to the other side. After this cold-blooded murder they had returned to drink at the pub without showing the slightest remorse. That civil war has brutalised and dehumanised not only the adults, but the children also. What must Jesus feel when he looks down on us? He must surely weep; as he wept for Jerusalem. It was gratifying to hear in that Assembly what efforts were being made by the Churches *together* to minister in that awful situation—how they were trying to heal the raw wounds of bigotry, hatred and bitterness, and how

88

they were being drawn together through their common ministry, perhaps more effectively than through all the debates they had had about Church unity. The Churches must beat their breasts in deep penitence for their part in helping to divide God's children into warring camps, instead of being agents of unity and justice and reconciliation. The dividedness of the Churches makes it difficult for people to believe in the Gospel of Jesus Christ.

Divided Churches are ineffective and wasteful. If we could pool our resources, we would be far more effective. Is it not wantonly wasteful of God's resources that each denomination must for instance build its own church, so that in one area, say of Soweto, there will be several church buildings belonging to rival denominations. Would it not be better to come together, and put up one or two structures which could be used by different denominations? The money saved could be used more effectively, to help feed the hungry, or to provide scholarships. It is a powerful argument—but it is ultimately not the real reason why the Christian Church should be one.

Some say the Churches are ineffective in their witness because they speak with many voices instead of one. When we met with the Prime Minister he said to what Church must he listen, since they all come to him, and speak differently when they do. President Samora Machel is reported to have told the Churches in Mozambique that he would listen to them only when they were united, speaking corporately and together. That again is a powerful argument, but it is not the real reason for our concern for Church unity.

The real reason is that our dividedness undermines the Gospel of Jesus Christ. He came to bring reconciliation; he broke down the middle wall of partition. How can we, the Church of God, say to a sadly divided world that we have the remedy for your animosities, your hatreds, your separateness, when we are ourselves so sinfully divided? Surely the world will retort, 'Physician heal thyself'. How can the Church, say in Northern Ireland, really preach reconciliation between the warring factions in that land, when Protestant and Roman Catholic are unable to share the bread of life together in Church?

What about us in South Africa? How can we say apartheid is evil and contrary to the Gospel of Love when we practise such a sad ecclesiastical apartheid? We have racially divided Churches, and we find all kinds of excuses to justify this. We say we are residentially segregated, or that there are language problems. We appoint our ministers on a racial basis. Whites can serve both black and white congregations, but only in the rarest situations have blacks ministered in white congregations. If they have done so, they have usually been assisted. Until recently our salaries were racially determined, and even now most of our multiracial Churches are really run by the minority—the whites. We have reflected our unjust and discriminatory society. Those who have been and still are victims of the injustice and oppression of apartheid, have seen the Churches as part of the oppressive system, especially because the privileged Christians have been crying 'Don't mix politics with religion' when some Christian leaders tried to condemn the evils of apartheid. These privileged Christians have helped to perpetuate the myth that Christianity is just something one does on Sunday, and has nothing to do with one's rent or housing or unemployment.

The credibility of the Gospel is at stake. We, the Church of God, can redeem ourselves if we are determined to work together as the Churches in Ulster, to witness together against injustice and oppression and exploitation, to stand together with the poor and the oppressed throughout the world, and here in South Africa with the victims of one of the most ruthless systems in the world. The credibility of the Gospel may be restored if we become the voice of the voiceless. God be praised that during the recent unrest in the schools, our Churches were seen to stand by the children, to act with them and on their behalf. To do this and all the other things I have suggested, is going to be costly. I fear that this government in South Africa is becoming more authoritarian, and that it will tolerate criticism and dissent less and less. Christian leaders who stand up to be counted in the struggle for justice, are going to get it in the neck. They will be harassed, they will be detained and arrested, they will be banned, and some will die mysteriously in detention. Many will just disappear from the face of the earth, as has happened in Russia, in the Iron Curtain countries, in Nazi Germany, in Amin's Uganda.

But we have no option, because we serve Him who said of himself:

'The Spirit of the Lord is upon me,
Because he has chosen me to bring
Good news to the poor.
He has sent me to proclaim liberty to the captives
and recovery of sight to the blind,
To set free the oppressed
And announce that the time has come
When the Lord will save his people.'

41. Women and the Church

Bishop Tutu here supports the growing movement that is campaigning for a balanced priesthood.

I BELIEVE we are, as male and female, an example of the interdependence of being human. The self-sufficient human person is in many ways sub-human. In Africa we say 'A person is a person through others'—one's humanity is interwoven with that of others. I believe that males and females have distinctive gifts, and both sets of gifts are indispensable for truly human existence. I am sure the Church has lost something valuable in denying ordination to women for so long. There is something uniquely valuable that women and men bring to the ordained ministry, and it has been distorted and defective as long as women have been debarred. Somehow men have been less human for this loss. But I would like to stress that women priests must not be tempted to emulate men priests. There will be many things where your sex will be an irrelevance in carrying out your ministry as an ordained person; but there are many other occasions when peculiarly feminine insights will be your unique and distinctive contribution. That is why I am myself unhappy that women priests dress like men

91

priests with dog collars. I know they have to assert that their priesthood is equal to that of men in all respects. But I would hope that they very quickly assert their self-assurance, and be women, not faint copies of men. They must not apologise for their existence, but celebrate their identity and personhood as women. That is what human liberation is all about. The Church and God's world need you as you, with your gentleness, your graciousness, your compassion.

There is something in the nature of God which corresponds to our maleness and our femaleness. We have tended to speak much more of the maleness, so we refer to the Fatherhood of God, which is as it should be. But we have missed out on the fullness that is God, when we have ignored that which corresponds to our femaleness. We have hardly spoken about the Motherhood of God, and consequently we have been the poorer for this.

I would like to refer to one aspect—a tremendous quality that women have—which relates to a like quality in God. It is the faith women have in people. Take a child who is a cause of much frustration and disillusion in others. The mother of that child can see the beauty and goodness hidden deep down, and women are much more patient than men in trying to bring that goodness to the surface. They have the capacity, more than men, to cherish that good and bring it to fruition. They are like the sculptor who can see the beautiful sculpture in a block of stone.

I think that is how God is—he has extraordinary patience with each one of us and sees us as we shall be. He brings to the surface the good that is hidden way down there and nurtures it, nurses it until it comes to full bloom. In many ways the manner in which Jesus handled Peter after the resurrection, is the way only God or a woman would. Peter, who had announced that he would follow Jesus to death, had not only denied him thrice, but had fled and abandoned him at the crucifixion. So he must have dreaded meeting Jesus after the resurrection. But notice the gentleness of Jesus. He asks Peter three times to declare he loves him, and three times gives him special responsibility—to cancel his threefold denial. That was believing in someone—affirming him so that he could have faith in himself.

Women, we need you to give us back our faith in humanity.

92

42. Children's Rights

From an address at a Home and Family Life Conference, at Hammanskraal during the Year of the Child, on 2 March 1979.

MY WIFE and I decided early on in our marriage, that we were going to try to let our children do a lot of things that we had been denied in our childhood. We had been brought up to know that children are meant to be seen and not heard. So as children we used to feel so terribly frustrated when those gods in our household—our parents and their grown-up friends—were discussing something really interesting. We were burning to ask 'who or what' in order to clarify some obscure point, but we never dared to interrupt.

I remember we were often warned not even to *look* at grown-ups as they were involved in some animated conversation. Living in cramped quarters, it was practically impossible to be interested in one's books, whilst people were laughing and joking in the same room. We were told to leave the room when other grown-ups came to visit our demigods, and we had to be quick about producing the tea (at any old hour), which the 'gods' enjoyed guzzling in enormous quantities. We had to be content with surreptitious swigs at the small hole in the condensed milk tin when no one was looking.

So we thought we did not want our children to go through all those traumas. Perhaps it was reinforced by the fact that we had moved to England, where our antiquated methods were things of the distant and hoary past. But it was not easy. I remember for instance saying to our youngest, who was then a very chirpy three-year-old, and quite sure that there were very few things that she did not know in the world: 'Mpho, darling, please keep quiet, you talk too much!' Do you think she was at all deflated by this rebuke? Not at all—quick as a shot she retorted: 'Daddy, you talk a lot too. You talk all by yourself in Church!' Well I never. One should not make light of what is called Culture Shock, for it is very real. There we were, Leah and I, utterly conditioned by our upbringing not to be sassy and talk back at adults, whilst our

93

children were in a culture where that is as normal as drinking tea. We were experiencing a new kind of trauma.

We stuck it out very painfully. We let them join in discussions with our adult friends—they interrupted, they argued, they contributed. I can tell you though, how we sometimes fumed, because one of our children had said: 'Oh Daddy, that's nonsense'. But we began to find that we had to relate to them as real persons, with points of view that had to be taken seriously. It was not enough to pull rank, and think it would suffice to say 'Do this'. 'Why?' they would ask. We had to begin to marshal facts to justify our position, not being merely authoritarian, although this might have made life less hectic from time to time.

Despite the traumas of belonging to two cultures, we know it was right to adopt the line we did. Children are a wonderful gift, and they are young and small persons, with minds and ideas, hating to be talked down at. They have an extraordinary capacity to see into the heart of things, and to expose sham and humbug for what they are. We must not idealise them too much, but I know that most of those I have had any dealings with respond wonderfully to being treated with respect, as persons who are responsible. There is the old saying: 'Give a dog a bad name and hang him'. If we treat our children as unreliable and dishonest why should we be surprised when they in fact behave as we reckon they would?

We are talking so much about liberation, about a just and participatory society, where decisions are not rammed down people's throats. We resent it, and quite rightly so, when people are forever letting us know what is good for us, when they are patronising or don't allow us to enjoy rights which we believe are inalienable, and which go with being human. But then in the society where we *can* do something about it, the home and family, we are a replica of the very society we condemn so roundly.

We discovered there was much fun in the home, and we parents developed as we pitted our strengths against those of our children. They were persons in their own right, and we had to think out many things that previously we had taken for granted. It did not mean letting go of discipline, because a rebellious child is really testing out the parameters of acceptable conduct, and that is part

94

of the painful process of growing up. And to have no standards that the family recognises, eventually means children have nothing to test themselves against. Pandering to him/her in the end turns out to be the worst thing you could do for them, and they will resent it for the rest of their lives, and you failed to help them grow up responsibly. After all, they were trying to get away from being known as the child of so-and-so. They were looking for self-esteem and self-identity. We know how much we hate as blacks and maybe as women (black and white) to have our identity determined in terms of another.

Let us work positively, so that we can contribute to the recognition of Children's Rights, and thereby work for a more just and equitable society, where everybody will have the right to a full life, to a stable family existence, to a free and compulsory education, to freedom of movement and association, to freedom from ignorance, hunger, and fear, and freedom of thought and worship.

43. Into the eighties

A press statement, released on 30 October 1979.

THE 1970s have been a decade of hope and despair. Hope because there has been so much concern about human freedom and rights around the world. Anyone flouting accepted standards of human rights could not do so with impunity. The whole world would be opposed to them. Much has been achieved in removing discrimination based on sex, colour, race and religion. But it has been a decade which has also seen people like Amin, Bokassa and others. There has been the ghastly spectacle of man's inhumanity to man in the Middle East, in the Far East, in Africa. We have seen a horrible increase in refugees the world over—in an affluent world there has been abject poverty and starvation, exploitation and oppression. But we believe it is God's world, and that one day his will for all of us will prevail. And so we go into the 1980s with a quiet confidence and optimism.

PART SIX

No Hands But Your Hands

The final section looks at the work of Desmond Tutu during the 1980s, the decade which saw him rise to world prominence as a courageous and resourceful opponent of apartheid, becoming the Nobel Peace Laureate and the Archbishop of Cape Town. He appeals to a worldwide audience, through sermons, speeches and statements, for assistance in bringing apartheid to an end.

44. Ambassador of Christ: the addresss to the United Nations Security Council

At the beginning of the 1980s the SACC was under investigation by a government-sponsored body—the Eloff Commission—in an obvious attempt to discredit the Church group which had become such a thorn in the side of the white minority government. The attempt, however, ended in miserable failure, with Bishop Tutu making a stirring defence of the Council, and its work continued as before.

The political protests which, despite brutal repression, have always continued in the face of apartheid, put increasing pressure on the South African regime and forced it to introduce a 'New Constitution' in September 1984, which gave Indian and Coloured people a small voice in Parliament. The black majority, sensing yet another 'divide and rule' policy, reacted with fury, and black unrest and brutal police repression became almost daily events.

It was at this point that the Nobel Peace Prize Committee, meeting in Oslo, voted to award Bishop Tutu the Nobel Peace Prize, in recognition of his efforts to bring peaceful social change to South Africa. Bishop Tutu heard the news in the USA, where he was staying on sabbatical, and was invited to address a UN Security Council meeting on South Africa. What follows is the slightly edited text of his address.

MR PRESIDENT, I am very deeply humbled by the honour which has been bestowed on me. I thank you for the privilege of addressing this gathering. I thank you for this opportunity most warmly, on my own behalf and on behalf of millions in my land who have been rendered voiceless, the marginalised ones.

It is one of the ironies of our South African situation that I would be denied in my home country the chance of addressing its highest representative body, but more of that a little later. I speak out of a full heart, for I am about to speak about a land that I love deeply and passionately—a beautiful land of rolling hills and gurgling streams, of clear starlit skies, of singing birds and gambolling lambs; a land God has richly endowed with the good things of the earth, a land rich in mineral deposits of nearly every kind, a land of vast open spaces, enough to accommodate all its inhabitants comfortably, a land capable of feeding itself and other lands on the beleaguered continent of Africa, a veritable bread-basket; a land that could contribute wonderfully to the material and spiritual development of all Africa and indeed of the whole world.

And so we would expect that such a land, veritably flowing with milk and honey, should be a land where peace and harmony and contentment reigned supreme. Alas, the opposite is the case. For my beloved country is wracked by division, by alienation, by animosity, by separation, by injustice, by avoidable pain and suffering. It is a deeply fragmented society, hagridden by fear and anxiety, covered by a pall of despondency and a sense of desperation, split up into hostile, warring factions. It is a highly volatile land, and its inhabitants sit on a powder-keg with a very short fuse indeed. There is endemic unrest, like a festering sore which will not heal until not just the symptoms are treated but the root causes are removed.

South African society is deeply polarised. Nothing illustrates this more sharply than the events of the past week. Whilst the black community was in the seventh heaven of delight because of the decision of that Committee in Oslo, and whilst the world was congratulating the recipient of the Nobel Peace Prize, the white government and most white South Africans, very sadly, were seeking to devalue that prize. An event which should have been the occasion of uninhibited joy and thanksgiving revealed a sadly divided society.

Before I came to this country, in early September, to go on Sabbatical, I visited one of the trouble-spots near Johannesburg. I went with members of the South African Council of Churches, which had met in emergency session after I had urged Mr P. W. Botha to meet with Church leaders to deal with a rapidly deteriorating situation. As a result of our peace initiative, we did get to meet with two cabinet ministers, demonstrating thereby our concern to carry out our call to be ministers of reconciliation and ambassadors of Christ. In this black township we met an old lady who told us that she was looking after her grandchildren and the children of neighbours whilst they were at work. On the day about which she was speaking, the police had been chasing black schoolchildren in that street, but the children had eluded the police, who then drove down the street past the old lady's house. Her wards were playing in front of the house, in the yard. She was sitting in the kitchen at the back, when her daughter burst in, calling agitatedly for her. She rushed out into the living room. A grandson had fallen just inside the door, dead. The police had shot him in the back. He was six years old. Recently a baby, a few weeks old, became the first white casualty of the current uprisings.

No death can leave us cold. Every death diminishes us. Every death is one too many. Those whom the black community has identified as collaborators with a system that oppresses them and denies them the most elementary human rights have met with cruel death, which we deplore as much as any others. They have rejected these people working within the system, whom they have seen as lackeys and stooges, despite their titles of town councillors, and so on, under an apparently new dispensation extending the right of local government to the blacks.

Over 100,000 black students are out of school, boycotting, as they did in 1976, what they and the black community perceive as an inferior education designed deliberately for inferiority. An already highly volatile situation has been ignited several times and, as a result, over 80 persons have died. There has been industrial unrest, with the first official strike by black miners taking place, not without its toll of fatalities among the blacks.

Some may be inclined to ask—but why should all this unrest be taking place just when the South African government appears to have embarked on the road of reform, exemplified externally by the signing of the Nkomati accord and internally by the implementation of a new constitution which appears to depart radically from the one it replaces, for it makes room for three chambers: one for whites, one for Coloureds, and one for Indians—a constitution described by many as a significant step forward?

I wish to state here, as I have stated on other occasions, that Mr P. W. Botha must be commended for his courage in declaring that the future of South Africa could no longer be determined by whites only. That was a very brave thing to do. The tragedy of

South Africa is that something with such a considerable potential for resolving the burgeoning crisis of our land should be vitiated by the exclusion of 73% of the population, the overwhelming majority in the land. By no stretch of the imagination could that kind of constitution be considered to be democratic. The composition of the committees, in the ratio of four whites to two Coloureds to one Indian, demonstrates eloquently what most people had suspected all along: that it was intended to perpetuate the rule of a minority. The fact that the first qualification for membership of the chambers is racial says that this constitution was designed to entrench racism and ethnicity. The most obnoxious features of apartheid would remain untouched and unchanged. The Group Areas Act, the Population Registration Act, separate educational systems for the different race groups; all this and more would remain quite unchanged.

This constitution was seen by the mainline English-speaking churches and the official white opposition as disastrously inadequate, and they called for its rejection in the whites-only referendum last November. The call was not heeded. The blacks overwhelmingly rejected what they regarded as a sham, an instrument in the politics of exclusion. Various groups campaigned for a boycott of the Coloured and Indian elections—campaigned, I might add, against very great odds, by and large peacefully. As we know, the authorities responded with their usual iron-fist tactics, detaining most of the leaders of the United Democratic Front (UDF) and other organisations that had organised the boycott.

The current unrest was in very large measure triggered off by the reaction of the authorities to anti-election demonstrations in August. The farcical overall turnout of only about 20% says more eloquently than anything else that the Indians and Coloureds have refused to be co-opted as the junior partners of apartheid—the phrase used by Allan Boesak.

There is little freedom in this land of plenty. As blacks we often run the gauntlet of roadblocks on roads leading into our townships. The authorities have not stopped stripping blacks of their South African citizenship. Here I am, 53 years old, a bishop in the Church, some would say reasonably responsible: I travel on a document that says my nationality is 'undeterminable at present'. The South African government is turning us into aliens in the land of our birth. It continues unabated with its vicious policy of forced population removals. It treats carelessly the women in the KTC squatter camp near Cape Town whose flimsy plastic coverings are destroyed every day by the authorities—and their heinous crime is that they want to be with their husbands, with the father of their children.

We ask you, please help us; urge the South African authorities to go to the conference table with the authentic representatives of all sections of our community. I appeal to this body to act. I appeal in the name of the ordinary, the little people of South Africa. I appeal in the name of the squatters in Crossroads and in the KTC camp. I appeal on behalf of the father who has to live in a single-sex hostel as a migrant worker, separated from his family for eleven months of the year. I appeal on behalf of the students who have rejected this travesty of education made available only for blacks. I appeal on behalf of those who are banned arbitrarily, who are banished, who are detained without trial, those imprisoned because they have had a vision of a new South Africa. I appeal on behalf of those who have been exiled from their homes.

I say we will be free, and we ask you: help us, that this freedom come for all of us in South Africa, black and white, but that it come with the least possible violence, that it come peacefully, that it come soon.

45. International intervention

As the year of 1984 came to a close, Bishop Tutu continued his efforts to bring apartheid to a peaceful conclusion. In the US he met with President Ronald Reagan, and tried to budge him from his policy of 'constructive engagement'. During their meeting Bishop Tutu showed him his travel document with its bizarre description of his nationality as 'Undetermined at present'; President Reagan, whose knowledge of South African history Tutu later described as 'horrible', was apparently shocked by this.

In fact, US policy towards South Africa at that time was dictated by Realpolitik rather than ethical values, and Tutu's appeals to the President were almost completely fruitless. However, his speeches and television appearances in the USA did contribute to a wave of anti-apartheid protests there, and many people, including well-known personalities, courted arrest to bring attention to the evils of apartheid. At last President Reagan was forced to respond to the pressure on him by introducing limited economic sanctions.

On 10 December 1984 Bishop Tutu was formally awarded the Nobel Peace Prize in Oslo, and after returning in triumph to South Africa he became Bishop of Johannesburg; he now had a prominent platform from where he could speak up for the aspirations of the black population. There was to be no let up in the chaos caused by apartheid; in 1985 unrest in South Africa escalated, and on the anniversary of Sharpeville 21 people were massacred by the police. This was the year of the infamous 'Trojan Horse' incident, when a group of police were captured on film provoking an incident with stone-throwing black youngsters, and then leaping from their hiding places on a lorry to shoot and kill their young opponents.

Asked by BBC Radio whether he thought anything had changed in South Africa since the days of the Sharpeville massacre, he replied in the negative. 'In 1960 I was a theological student, and the then Bishop of Johannesburg Ambrose Reeves was in the thick of things. All these years later the Bishop of Johannesburg is having to be running around trying to douse fires, when he and everybody knows that we are not likely to have true security and stability until apartheid has been done away with.'

In July 1985 he tried to stem the grim development of black people killing blacks thought to be collaborators with the security forces: he was seen on worldwide television rescuing a suspected informer from the wrath of an angry crowd, and also, a fortnight later, telling a large gathering that he would leave South Africa unless such killings came to an end.

Other developments included the loss of government authority in the townships, consumer boycotts of the white economy, and police attacks on schools and township residents; in July the government imposed a 'State of Emergency' on the country. Under its provisions 10,000 people were detained, many of whom were tortured in police custody, and reporting restrictions were introduced. After the worldwide revulsion that followed the screening of television pictures of police action in the townships, television coverage of events there was prohibited, so that—as Jesse Jackson put it—'they can do their killing and murdering and lynching in the dark'.

Towards the end of this dark year Bishop Tutu visited Britain to take part in preparations for the 1988 Lambeth conference. On 7 October he addressed a meeting at the Royal Commonwealth Society in London, reviewing the history of apartheid, exposing the deceitful strategies that the apartheid regime had used to fend off world disapproval, and calling for increased pressure from the Western world to bring apartheid to an end. The following is the edited text of that address.

I CAME on what has been billed as a private visit to prepare for Lambeth 1988. When Lambeth happens in that year it will have been—or will be—the fortieth anniversary of the advent of apartheid in South Africa. Will there still be apartheid—a system as vicious, as evil, as unchristian, as totally immoral as Nazism ever was—in 1988?

In my view the answer to that question depends very much on what the West, especially Britain, the United States and West Germany, choose to do or not to do. In the black view they have provided a kind of *cordon sanitaire* for Mr P. W. Botha against the consequences of his extraordinary policies. He has known that he could rely on the protection of these countries at the United Nations when the Security Council has voted on some form of action against South Africa. One of them would certainly veto or firmly declare its opposition to that action, or whatever other action would be likely to end apartheid.

The apartheid system has developed through a number of stages. The first step was one of the blatant naked racism where they were making no bones at all about the fact that they intended to keep the 'Native' very firmly in his place. We were the 'Native' with a capital N and those were the days when they went around with pictures of an unkempt 'Native' asking in conspiratorial tones: 'Would you like your daughter to marry this man?' As you probably know blacks now have their retort which is: 'Show us your daughter first!'

When the government realised that apartheid had attracted the opposition it so richly deserved it tried to produce something that would appear to give apartheid a new face, a moral justification. And so there arose things peculiar to South Africa like 'parallel democracies', 'separate development', 'plural democracy'. We were then called 'plurals'—so one of us I suppose was a 'singular plural' and those in the country must have been 'rural plurals'. They then came up with this idea about the bantustans, based on the theory that South Africa is not a country where there is a minority facing up to an overwhelming majority. Oh no, the government said: 'We are a nation of minorities, and the whites—French, German, English, Portuguese, Spanish, whatever —are able by some wonderful alchemy to cohere and form one nation, but you blacks are actually split up into different nations'. We say: 'Now could you possibly explain to us by what *tour de force* it is possible that you cohere in this kind of way, and we do not?' They don't answer that. Their aim was to denationalise us, to turn us into aliens in the land of our birth.

That's smart. You have to hand it to them: aliens cannot claim many rights in whatever country he is an alien, least of all political rights. There then followed this extraordinary business when they went around destroying stable black communities in order to satisfy this racist ideology of theirs; three-and-a-half million people were uprooted and dumped as if they were rubbish in arid poverty-stricken 'homelands', the father then having to leave his family eking out a miserable existence while he comes into the white man's town and lives for eleven months of the year in a single sex hostel. This undermined black family life, not accidentally but deliberately, in a country which has a public holiday dedicated to the sanctity of family life called Family Day. It happens in a country which claims to be the last bastion of Western Christian white civilisation.

And then the West comes along and tells us that these ought to be our friends. The government of South Africa has many amongst it who during the Second World War supported the Nazis, while our fathers and brothers and uncles were the ones who were facing up to Rommel's Desert Rats with assegais, because Smuts said blacks should not be armed. Our people died in order to try to save Western civilisation, and now the allies of the West are those who at the time sought to see Hitler prevail. You know, you say to them 'release Nelson Mandela' and they say 'no, he must renounce violence'—the first person the Nationalist government released in 1948 was Robbie Liebrandt, who had been sentenced to death on a charge of high treason for assisting the Nazis.

There's a poignant story of a black gardener who had been working in Johannesburg, who wasn't getting a very high salary but got enough money to build a very decent house for himself back home. One day he was told that this community had to move, and that this house was one of those which had to be demolished. This man said, 'Will you please allow me to demolish my own house?' and they allowed him to. The following morning they found him hanging from a tree. That's the kind of price apartheid exacts—it's too exorbitant. That was the second phase.

Then we arrived at the phase of the 'New Constitution', in fact a very logical development of the politics of exclusion. Apartheid has been basically a matter of maintaining power over the vast majority of the people, done by preventing access to political power, which gives access to all other kinds of power. With political power one can then determine that 20% of the population will then have 87% of the land, and that 80% of the population will have the remaining 13%. You can then spend ten times the amount on the education of a black child, and decree that there should be separate residential areas.

Now we are told that we are in the year of reform. Dr Koornhof once said that apartheid has died; we said 'That's a very interesting observation—could someone please show us the corpse and have the decency to invite us to the funeral?' In our experience apartheid is not dead—apartheid is as powerful as it ever was. In the 'year of reform', when they now have Indian and so-called 'coloured' Parliamentarians they couldn't use the dining hall in the Houses of Parliament because it had been set aside for whites only. In this 'year of reform' our people die when they try to

107

oppose the system peacefully. You have seen the kind of brutality that has occurred when peaceful demonstrations in the tradition of our people have been mounted. From the foundation of the African National Congress in 1912 till the day that it was banned in 1960 it used conventional methods—demonstrations, petitions, passive resistance—yet what happened? In 1960 sixty-nine people protesting peacefully against the Pass Laws were killed, shot in the back most of them, running away. Our children go around singing in the streets in 1976 and what happens? Over 500 people get killed.

What must we do that we have not done? What must we say that we have not said? Does it matter to you that three-year-olds are killed with police rubber bullets? Or does it not matter because—well, it isn't really children, it's black children. Does it matter to you that the police can go out and kick girls—teenagers—in the face so that the girl loses five teeth? What must we say, what language must we use that would make you understand? We have a *cri de coeur*—all we are saying is 'do you recognise that we are human?' Does it matter to you that a thousand of our people have been killed since August of last year? Or is it swatting flies? Would you and your governments and all these wonderful people have the same kind of equanimity and debate in a kind of detached academic way—'Well you know sanctions . . . yes well no . . . the people who will suffer first of all are blacks'—ha ha ha. How wonderfully altruistic. Through all this time I haven't heard a squeak of concern about black suffering, and now suddenly all these wonderful people come and tell us that 'if we apply sanctions you will suffer'. They're talking about a future possible suffering—they don't say much about our actual suffering now.

Some people say that they are very concerned to see change, and we reply that there are three ways in which this can come about. You can vote people out of power (we can't use that, we don't have the vote), you can use violence (we say actually we don't want to use violence), so we are left with the peaceful option—but when you canvass methods that are likely to bring about change you discover that people like change as long as things remain the same.

Now my dear friends, let me not give you the impression that it is black people only in South Africa who want to see change. White South Africans are not demons. It would be so much more simple to say 'oh if you look at them carefully you can see that they have horns and tails' and dismiss them like that. But you can't—they are ordinary human beings, most of them very scared. You would be too if you were outnumbered 5 to 1 and always thinking in racial categories. They are always thinking 'if once we let go having treated these blacks as we have . . .'. They then transfer to us how they would have reacted if they had been treated as they have been treating us. But there are some wonderful white people, and I often say that I would need a lot of grace if I was white to oppose the system which provides me with such substantial privileges just because I am white. Those white people—and there are many—who are opposed to apartheid in our country need to be commended even more warmly than us blacks.

Let me finish by saying dear friends you still have a chance of making a moral decision, because it is a moral decision, a moral issue that is facing you. Are you or are you not in favour of oppression and injustice? On which side are you really? Don't you think your best interests will be served by siding quite firmly with those who will be running this country? Because there is no question that we are going to be free. We are not debating that. If anyone wants to debate that I'm sorry—we are going to be free. We would like that freedom to come peacefully, by negotiation, and that is what we have turned most of our energies into doing. Or are we going to be free through chaos, through violence, through bloodshed—and there's already a lot of that happening at home. But there is still the possibility of peaceful change if your governments apply the kind of pressure we ask them to. They should say to the South African government 'unless you do so-and-so (and here are the so-and-so's) then we are going to act'. There should be a demand that the South African government dismantle apartheid—no equivocation—release all political prisoners and detainees, allow all exiles who want to do so to return home and then sit down and talk.

For we have a great country. Can you imagine when all the

109

energy and resources that are at present invested in either upholding apartheid or opposing it will be turned to working for all of us? What a tremendous country it will be when black and white will be holding hands and striding forth into this glorious future the vistas of which God is letting open in front of us. What a wonderful South Africa it will be when people will count—all of us, black and white—because all of us are of infinite worth, because all of us are created in the image of God. When that land will be the launching pad not just for Southern Africa but for the whole of the continent, to propel it into the twenty-first century. I hope to invite you to the celebrations of our liberation.

46. The Delmas trial

At another visit to Britain, again taking part in preparations for the Lambeth Conference, Tutu, now Archbishop Tutu, organised the following message to be sent to the accused in the Delmas trial. The trial was an example of South Africa's notorious 'treason trials', and the defendants, along with United Democratic Front leaders, included Thom Manthatha, staff member of the South African Council of Churches. The trial, the longest treason trial in South African history, took place over a four-year period, from 1984 to 1988.

PLEASE TELEX TO JOHANNESBURG SOUTH AFRICA

To those accused in the Delmas Trial.

We assure you of our love and prayers as your case resumes in Pretoria. We pray that justice will prevail in your case as well as in your country. God protect you and your families.

Signed: Archbishop Desmond Tutu and forty-one members of the

Anglican communion, meeting at St Augustine's seminar, preparing for the 1988 Lambeth Conference.

ENDS MESSAGE

Seven of the eighteen defendants, including Thom Manthatha, were convicted; Manthatha received a six-year term of imprisonment. However, the sentences were overturned on appeal in December 1989.

47. South Africa and the African continent

In 1986 Bishop Tutu had been elected to the highest office in the Anglican Church of South Africa—the Archbishopric of Cape Town. Two months before the formal enthronement he sharply criticised President Reagan, who had again opposed the worldwide movement for imposing economic sanctions against the apartheid regime.

Despite another series of hollow reforms initiated by the Botha government, Tutu had begun to defy South African law by calling openly for economic sanctions to be imposed by the international community. Commenting on two non-violent campaigns which had brought about social change relatively peacefully—Gandhi's Satyagraha campaign in India and the Civil Rights movement in the USA headed by Martin Luther King—he said on BBC Radio that in South Africa it might not be possible to emulate their success.

'Passive resistance and non-violent action', he said, 'presume a certain minimum moral level, so that Gandhi knew there were people in England who would be morally outraged at the things the British troops were doing, and would therefore agitate for change. I'm not certain that in South Africa we have that minimum moral level.'

As for the Civil Rights movement in the USA: 'There is one fundamental difference—the law in the USA was on the side of those campaigning then. What Martin Luther King and those with him were doing was to reclaim rights that were theirs under the Constitution. Here we do not have the support of the Constitution or the law.'

It is easy then to understand Bishop Tutu's anger at the threadbare arguments of Western leaders against economic sanctions— following President Reagan's anti-sanctions speech, he declared that 'the West can go to hell'. Other leaders of the South African black community support the call for sanctions, declaring, in the words of a United Democratic Front spokesman, that sanctions 'will help the interests of our people', and—according to Walter Sisulu—that 'sanctions have helped to bring about what little change there has been'. If put to a referendum opinion polls indicate that sanctions would be overwhelmingly endorsed by South African blacks.

This press statement from 1987 was made following a visit by white liberal leader Dr Van Zyl Slabbert to discuss the South African situation with members of the exiled African National Congress in Dakar.

IN OUR struggle for justice, peace and reconciliation in South Africa, we owe a great deal to you ladies and gentlemen of the media, for we depend so much on arousing the moral outrage of the world community at the horrors and viciousness of apartheid. We go on hoping that the international community will assist us to dismantle the diabolical system of apartheid, which has inflicted and continues to inflict so much totally unnecessary suffering on God's children, just because they happen to be black.

We need the intervention of the international community because of our commitment to a non-violent and peaceful resolution of the crisis in our land. The South African government, which has often claimed not really to care two hoots about international opinion, has shown it fears the power of publicity by the severe curbs it has placed on the media. I would have thought that the spectacle of 'necklacing' widely shown on television would fill people with revulsion and some sympathy for the dilemmas facing the South African government. Clearly it can't be that they don't want the world to see something which would benefit the South African authorities.

Then one is led to believe that it is scared at the response of the world to scenes depicting the brutality and violence that the security forces unleash on men and women and young people protesting peacefully. The South African authorities are apprehensive of the reaction of the world to scenes of heavily armed police using their quirts on peaceful mourners at a funeral, or of police and soldiers armed to the teeth dispersing chanting pall-bearers with teargas, when the same police seem suddenly affected with a strange impotence in acting against the hooligans of the AWB (Afrikaner Weerstandsbewaging) who demonstrated at Jan Smuts Airport against the Dakar contingent who had gone to meet the ANC. These neo-Nazis of the AWB, let it be noted, mounted their demonstration after issuing dire threats to the Van Zyl Slabbert group, threats which if they had been made, say, by a black group against a white delegation would certainly not have been treated with the same police equanimity.

Primary violence

I WANT to reiterate yet again my own personal commitment to work for justice and peace in our land non-violently. As before, I now say again in the light of last week's bomb explosion in Johannesburg that I condemn such acts without equivocation, for I condemn all violence as evil, whether it is the violence of an evil and vicious system such as apartheid, or that of those who wish to overthrow such an unjust and repressive system.

I need to underline that the South African situation is already violent, since violence is inherent in the very nature of apartheid; that violence is not introduced *de novo* from outside by those called terrorists, but that the primary violence—and this is something the world must acknowledge and act against—the primary violence in South Africa is that of apartheid and its perpetrators. It is the violence of forced population removals, when people, God's children, are dumped as if they were things, as if they were rubbish, in poverty-stricken bantustan homeland resettlement camps. It is the violence of detention without trial, accompanied, as this practice often seems to be, by torture and solitary confinement (which is an exquisite form of torture). It is

113

the violence of detaining without trial even children as young as eleven years old. On the government's own admission there were over four hundred children detained in the last state of emergency, most of whom were released with no charge against them. The police have been acting as prosecutors and judges in their own case.

I could multiply examples of the violence of apartheid to which our people have constantly over the years responded non-violently until their political organisations were banned in 1960, when many said they had no option but to undertake the armed struggle. This was after events such as Sharpeville, when sixty-nine peaceful demonstrators were killed, many shot in the back. Nelson Mandela (who has just turned sixty-nine, after twenty-five years in jail) and others were only trying to assert that they were human, demanding to be treated as human beings. The system could not tolerate their temerity.

So I want to express my sympathies with those who were in the latest bomb outrage in Johannesburg. At the same time, it is important to underline the violence of apartheid and to arouse the world's anger against it. Recently the police were involved in a black township in Port Elizabeth with a man they claimed was an ANC so-called terrorist. At the end of their operation they bulldozed a shack in which the man was, crushing him and a woman companion. Now what evidence did they have that she was his collaborator, even if they were correct about his being an ANC insurgent? And supposing there had been innocent children in that shack—would it have meant nothing to have killed them? There was no outcry from those in South Africa who claim to be opposed to violence. Equally, when innocent civilians in the neighbouring front-line states of Southern Africa are killed in South African Defence Force raids, no real outrage is expressed.

Our people even now try to use non-violent methods to protest against apartheid. They use means such as the rent boycott: you saw last night the cruel response of the authorities in their callous eviction of people even in the middle of a bitterly cold winter. Our people are peaceloving to a fault.

114

Mozambique

Here Archbishop Tutu comments on the situation in Mozambique, one of South Africa's neighbours. One of the cruellest manifestations of apartheid in the 1980s was the South African attempt to destabilise her newly independent neighbours, often desperately poor, beset by colossal problems, and urgently requiring a period of peace to recover from their struggles for independence.

The plight of the Mozambican people has been one result of South African strategic manoeuvring in the region. Despite signing the Nkomati accord with President Samora Machel of Mozambique (by which South Africa and Mozambique promised not to interfere in each other's internal affairs), South Africa has continued to support an insurgent movement inside Mozambique, Renamo (MNR), which has caused immense suffering inside the country. A particularly brutal example of this was the Homoine massacre, when a group of MNR fighters slaughtered an entire village.

I AM challenging the government of South Africa to come clean: do they support the MNR bandits or don't they? We saw some of the victims of atrocities committed by the MNR on our last visit to Mozambique—in one hospital a man whose head had been nearly severed by Renamo had had it sewn back again, back and front. We saw a baby shot in the head, with the bullet nearly missing its brain. What we saw were instances of naked terrorism, which have now culminated in the Homoine massacre of nearly four hundred innocent Mozambicans in the same region that we visited. If the South African government supports Renamo then it supports terrorism, and must be condemned by Western governments as sharply as any other terrorist supporter.

The plight of Mozambique is due almost entirely to apartheid. I call on the international community:

(A) to step up dramatically its efforts to destroy apartheid before apartheid destroys us in the Republic of South Africa and the sub-continent.

(B) to pour aid into Mozambique to alleviate what has been

called a man-made crisis. I want to commend Mrs Thatcher and her government for increased British aid to Mozambique, as well as the outstanding work of the British aid agencies, especially the Disasters Emergency Committee. The victims are enormously grateful for this assistance. I would hope Mrs Thatcher would see that there is much the same sort of human misery in South Africa, and take characteristically decisive action.

We believe that economic action on the part of the international community still represents our last chance for a reasonably peaceful end to apartheid. It is interesting that COSATU (the Congress of South African Unions) in its last annual conference representing black workers still advocated sanctions as the last chance to help end apartheid. We call on international banks not to roll over loans until specific political conditions are met—an end to the State of Emergency, the release of detainees and political prisoners and a willingness to engage in real talks about dismantling apartheid with the authentic leaders and representatives of the people.

Lastly, I just want to say about Dr Van Zyl Slabbert's initiative that it is always good for people to talk rather than fight. But we must not overrate the significance of the Dakar encounter. It will have helped some whites realise that the African National Congress is not a bunch of bloodthirsty vampires but patriotic South Africans who want a new non-racial democratic and just South Africa which would be a boon to the African continent and the free world.

Help us to achieve that goal, for your intervention is critical. (*4 August 1987*)

48. Text of telegram sent by Archbishop Tutu for the London première of *Cry Freedom*

Sir Richard Attenborough's film Cry Freedom, *based on the life and struggle of Steve Biko, was premièred in London on 26 November 1987. The film told how a sceptical newspaper editor, Donald Woods, met Biko and began to see South Africa through his eyes, leaving the little world of the white South African and becoming aware of the true nature of South African society.*

During the 1980s the Western world's artistic community has by and large responded magnificently to apartheid. In the field of music the commitment to the cultural boycott of South Africa was resoundingly endorsed by an American coalition of musicians, 'Artists against Apartheid', and the sense of sorrow and waste at Steve Biko's murder by the South African police was hauntingly captured by Peter Gabriel's song, 'Biko'.

These efforts culminated in the 'birthday party' held in Wembley stadium in the summer of 1988, to celebrate the seventieth birthday of the imprisoned Nelson Mandela. Stars from Britain and the US attended, and a whole day of entertainment was rounded off by American opera singer Jessye Norman, who sang 'Amazing Grace'. The event drew a global audience, being televised live throughout the world.

The following message from Archbishop Tutu reveals the importance he places on this kind of response to apartheid, demonstrated by Cry Freedom. *It was read out to the audience before the film was screened.*

I GREET you in the name of those who are struggling for justice and peace in our beautiful but sad land. I am sorry not to have been able to be present at what must be a deeply significant occasion. I want to congratulate Sir Richard Attenborough and all who have been associated with him in producing this film. The South African government has imposed very severe curbs on the media to prevent any real news about what is happening in our country getting out to the world or even to South Africans. I welcome this

117

film especially for being able to focus the attention of the world on an evil and vicious system that must be dismantled so that black and white will be able to live together as God intends. God bless you all.

49. Lambeth—resolutions on South Africa

At the 1988 Lambeth Conference, where Anglican Church leaders and workers from all over the world met to discuss Church issues, Archbishop Tutu was appointed Vice-Chairman of the group which met to discuss 'Christianity and the Social Order'. The grouping sponsored a resolution on South Africa, which read as follows, and was adopted by the conference.

39. South Africa

This conference:
1. Re-affirms its belief that the system of apartheid in South Africa is evil and especially repugnant because of the cruel way a tyrannical racist system is being upheld in the name of the Christian faith.
2. Condemns the detention of children without just cause.
3. Calls upon the Churches to press their governments to:
   (A) bring the maximum pressure to bear on the South African regime in order to promote a genuine process of change towards the establishment of democratic political structures in a unified state;
   (B) institute forms of sanction calculated to have the maximum effect in bringing an end to the evil dispensation, and in establishing a just peace among all citizens;
   (C) give direct aid to anti-apartheid organisations within South Africa particularly with a view to assisting the unemployed and persecuted.

(D) give effective practical support to the Frontline States in order to ensure their economic survival and welfare, as well as their military protection from the threat of South African aggression;

(E) push for the release of Nelson Mandela and all other political prisoners and detainees in South Africa, and the unbanning of organisations like the African National Congress and the Pan-Africanist Congress which represent the majority of citizens;

(F) give direct moral and humanitarian support to such organisations in the pursuit of a just order which reflects gospel values and urges the Churches to ensure that none of their own financial resources is used to support the present regime in South Africa, and for this purpose to disinvest from all corporations which have a significant financial stake in South Africa.

4. Believes that to work for a just peace in South Africa is to work for the true liberation of all peoples of the region, black and white.

The Lambeth Conference also saw an attempt to define the times when the use of violence is justified to bring about an end to tyranny. This clearly grew out of the South African experience, and read in part as follows:

27. War, Violence and Justice

This conference:

2. (A) Supports those who choose the way of non-violence as being the way of our Lord, including direct non-violent action . . .

(B) Understands those who, after exhausting all other ways, choose the way of armed struggle as the only way to justice, whilst drawing attention to the dangers and injustices possible in such action itself.

50. No hands but your hands

In June 1989 Archbishop Tutu visited Britain to attend the Surrexit conference, an Anglican gathering in Portsmouth. During his visit he symbolically washed the feet of twelve of the participants, and delivered this sermon on the theme of the social dimension of Christianity.

I WANT to thank you for your love and for your prayers, and for caring for us in our situation in Southern Africa—a situation of violence and injustice and oppression. It matters enormously, and it is wonderful to belong to the Church of God and to know yourselves upheld by the love of so many sisters and brothers round the world, most of whom we shall not see this side of death.

You might recall how the prophet Zechariah speaks of the new, the restored Jerusalem, that it will be so populous that it won't have conventional walls, and Yahweh, God, says: 'I will be a wall of fire round Jerusalem'. We who are in situations such as our own have experienced almost as a veritable physical thing this being upheld, and we know this wall of fire that surrounds us.

We have an extraordinary God, this one we worship. God the immortal, the invisible, the eternal and the omnipotent. He created all there is, including ourselves without our aid. And yet, paradoxically, this omnipotent and all powerful God has always wanted to wait on the collaboration of human partners to accomplish his purposes.

Presumably by definition, being omnipotent, God could if he had so wished, delivered the children of Israel from bondage on his own account—and yet he sought out a human co-worker. This seems to be how God has always wanted to operate. As you know, he had quite a business persuading Moses to undertake the commission . . . 'What me, go to Pharaoh—God, you can't be serious. I mean you know I am a stammerer.'

Humanly speaking, if Moses had succeeded in persuading God to try elsewhere, the Israelites might still have been in bondage in Egypt today. We could multiply examples of the reluctant co-workers God had to persuade to partner him. Mary could have said to the Archangel Gabriel, when he came to her and told her that God wanted her to become the mother of his son—'What, me?—not on your life. What will the village people think—they know everything about everybody. What will they think of me becoming an unmarried mother? No thank you, try next door.' Mercifully, wonderfully, she responded: 'Behold the handmaid of the Lord, be it unto me according to thy word', and the whole world, nay, the whole created order, breathed a cosmic sigh of relief.

Our God is the same yesterday, today and forever. God still is ready to jeopardise the success of whatever divine enterprise he undertakes. He is willing to limit the power and effectiveness by waiting on the willingness and ability of his human partners. God is as strong as the weakest of his frail collaborators. God is as successful as we care to make him.

You might have seen a collection of cartoons, entitled *My God*. One of them shows God looking at a poster that says 'God is dead', and saying 'Oh dear, that makes me feel a little insecure'. The one I want to refer to is one that shows God looking somewhat disconsolate—'oh dear, I seem to have lost my copy of the divine plan'. Looking at the state of the world, you may often wonder if he did have one!

Natural and man-made disasters, floods, earthquakes, the Holocaust, Chernobyl, ecological problems, unbelievable, unending queues of the casualties of our inhumanity to one another, the victims of injustice and oppression, of starvation—you name it, it's all there in so many parts of the world. Sectarian strife in Northern Ireland, in Afghanistan, in Sri Lanka, in Kampuchea, in the Sudan, in Ethiopia, in Iran and Iraq, on the West Bank and Gaza Strip, in South Africa, in Latin America, and more recently the awful things that have happened and are continuing to happen in China—the doleful catalogue seems endless, and we can say with considerable relief: Thank God I am not God, but then go on with even greater relief to say: Thank God you are God.

For our God is the God who cares, our God is the God who hears, our God is the God who knows, and when our God beholds the condition of his children our God comes down to deliver. Our God is God Immanuel. So that when a king throws three young

121

people into a fiery furnace, God doesn't shout good advice from a distance. God comes down and the king sees the people walking unharmed in the fire. Our God is there with us.

You recall the story from the concentration camps, of a Jew who had been taunted by his Nazi guard and was given the awful task of cleaning out the toilets; looking down on him the Nazi gloatingly said 'And where is your God now?' The Jew quietly said: 'He is right here with me in the muck'. This God, this self-emptying God, this God who always makes himself available to us, this vulnerable God, this weak God, this dying God, this God asks us to be his human co-workers—please help me transform all the evil of this world, its hatred, its animosity, its grasping competitiveness, its selfish hoarding of the good things of God's earth for just a few—please help me transform them, to transfigure them into their glorious opposites.

The world out there can be tough. People are being taken hostage; we think of Terry Waite and other people who are held in detention without trial, even young children as in South Africa, held incommunicado without access to their family, to doctors of their choice, or to lawyers. As we sit here people are being tortured; as we sit here people are being killed, people are being thrown out of work and made redundant as projects are seen to be more valuable than persons. As we sit here families are crowded in totally inadequate and decaying housing in depressed communities. And when you are poor and unemployed often it is suggested that that happens to you because you are somehow to blame: if you were not so shiftless you would not have landed in the pickle in which you find yourself.

There is a disturbing increase in the incidence of child and wife abuse, in domestic violence. People are taking what they think is the easy way out, they are taking drugs as they find it increasingly difficult to cope; they become hobos and dropouts, and they even commit suicide. Our societies tend to be harsh with those it regards as failures. People feel less and less valued for who they are—they are valued for what they can achieve—for the ethic of the rat-race holds sway when stomach ulcers are considered status symbols, while virtues such as compassion are despised by those who must succeed at all costs.

122

God says: my dear children, please help me, please be my partner for I have no hands except your hands, no feet except your feet, no eyes but your eyes to look out into the world. I ask you please tie a towel round your waist and wash the feet of my children. Please help me transform, transfigure this world so that there can be more justice, more caring, more compassion. Please tell them that I love them with a love that does not change. I love them with a love that does not depend on what they do or achieve. I love them, period—and that invests them with a value that is incalculable. I love them, each one of them, as though they were the only person around. I love them because they have become the sanctuary of the Divine Trinity. Tell them this. And tell those who would want to treat them as if they were less than this that what they do is not just wrong, not just evil—what they do when they treat a child of God as if they were less than this is a blasphemy, a sacrilege, for it is like spitting in the face of God.

Please go out on my behalf, says God, agitate for a more equitable world economic system where developing countries will be able to sell their raw materials for fair prices and won't be milked dry trying to pay heavy foreign debts. Please help me stop the horrendous arms race when obscene amounts are spent on instruments of death and destruction, when a small fraction of this would ensure that God's children everywhere would have a decent education, adequate housing, health, a clean supply of water and a healthy family life. Help me, help me create the kind of universe where my children of all races and colours can live harmoniously together as members of one family, the human family, my family.

God calls us to serve his world and so serve him who said: 'in as much as you have done this to the least of these my brothers and sisters, you have done it as to me'. God says help me, help me transfigure the kingdoms of this world so that they become as the kingdom of our God and of his Christ and he shall reign forever and ever.

123

Bibliography

No Easy Walk to Freedom. Articles, speeches and trial addresses of Nelson Mandela. Edited by Ruth First. Heinemann, 1980.

I Write What I Like. Steve Biko. A selection of his writings edited by Aelred Stubbs CR. Heinemann, 1979.

Steve Biko. A biography by Donald Woods. Paddington Press, 1978.

The Sun Will Rise. Statements from the dock by South African political prisoners (including Robert Sobukwe and Nelson Mandela). Edited by Mary Benson. International Defence and Aid Fund, 1976.

The Church Struggle for Justice in South Africa. J. W. de Gruchy. SPCK, 1979.

The Freedom Charter of South Africa 1955. Published by the United Nations Centre Against Apartheid.

Tutu—Voice of the Voiceless. A biography by Shirley du Boulay. Penguin, 1988.

124